KAISER CHI

'Employment'

"Made in Great Britain"

ISBN-13: 978-1-4234-2006-4
ISBN-10: 1-4234-2006-3

7777 W. Bluemound Rd. P.O. Box 13819 Milwaukee, WI 53213

In Australia Contact:
Hal Leonard Australia Pty. Ltd.
4 Lentara Court
Cheltenham, Victoria, 3192 Australia
Email: ausadmin@halleonard.com

Visit Hal Leonard Online at
www.halleonard.com

Everyday I Love You Less and Less

Words & Music by Nicholas Hodgson, Richard Wilson, Andrew White, James Rix & Nicholas Baines

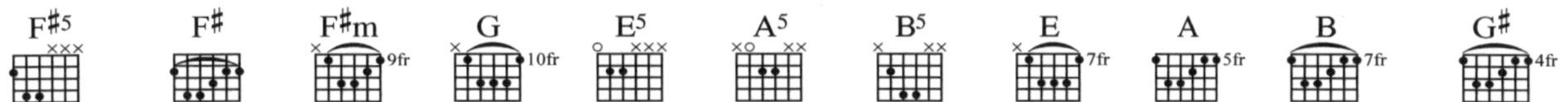

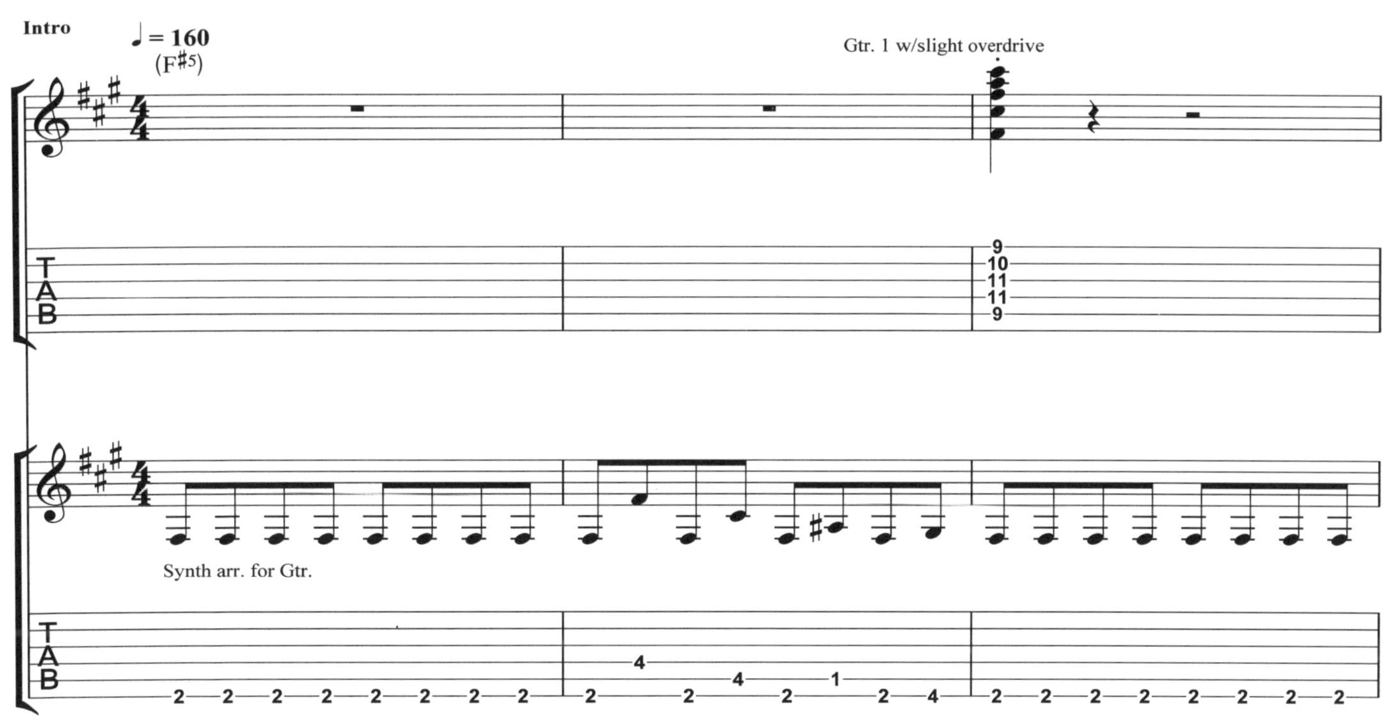

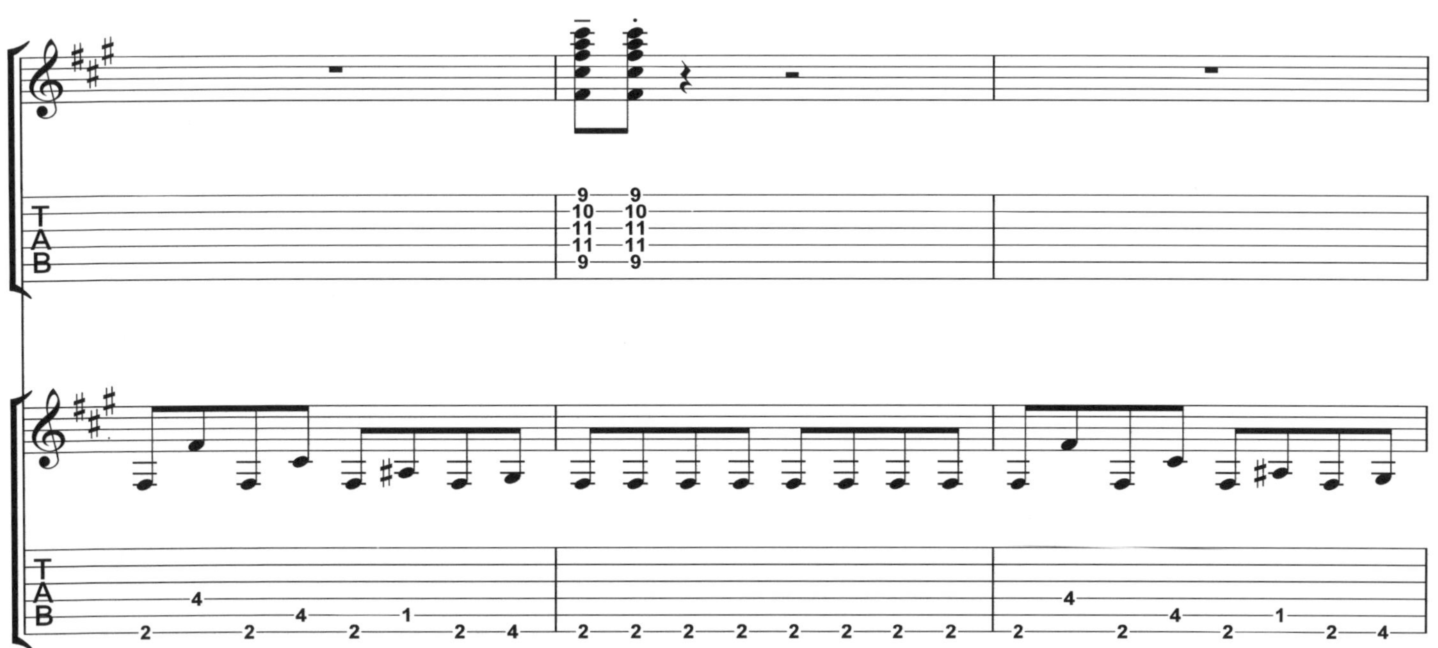

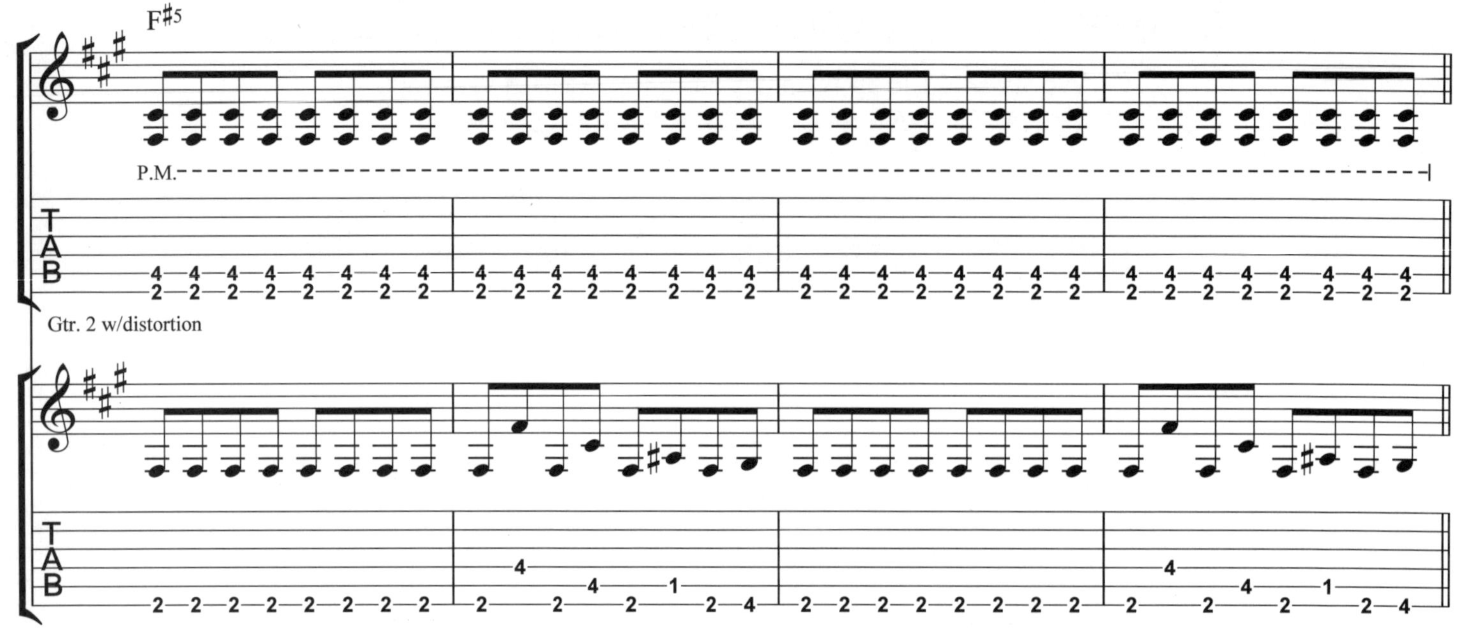
F♯5
P.M.
Gtr. 2 w/distortion

Verse
F♯5
Ev - 'ry day I love you less and less. It's clear to see that you've be - come ob -

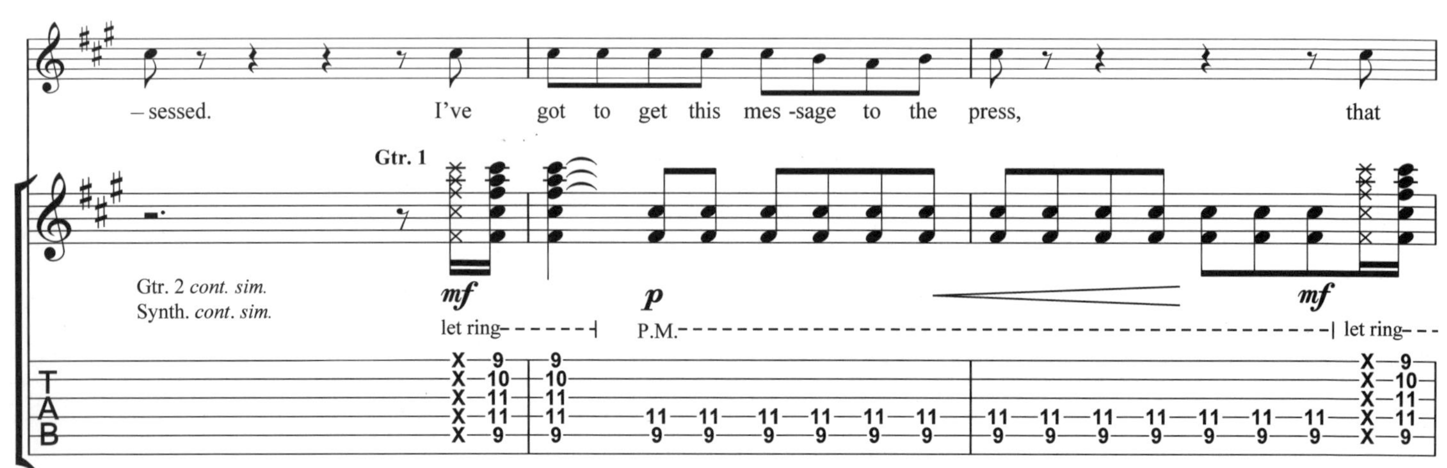
– sessed. I've got to get this mes - sage to the press, that
Gtr. 1
Gtr. 2 cont. sim.
Synth. cont. sim.
mf
p
let ring
P.M.

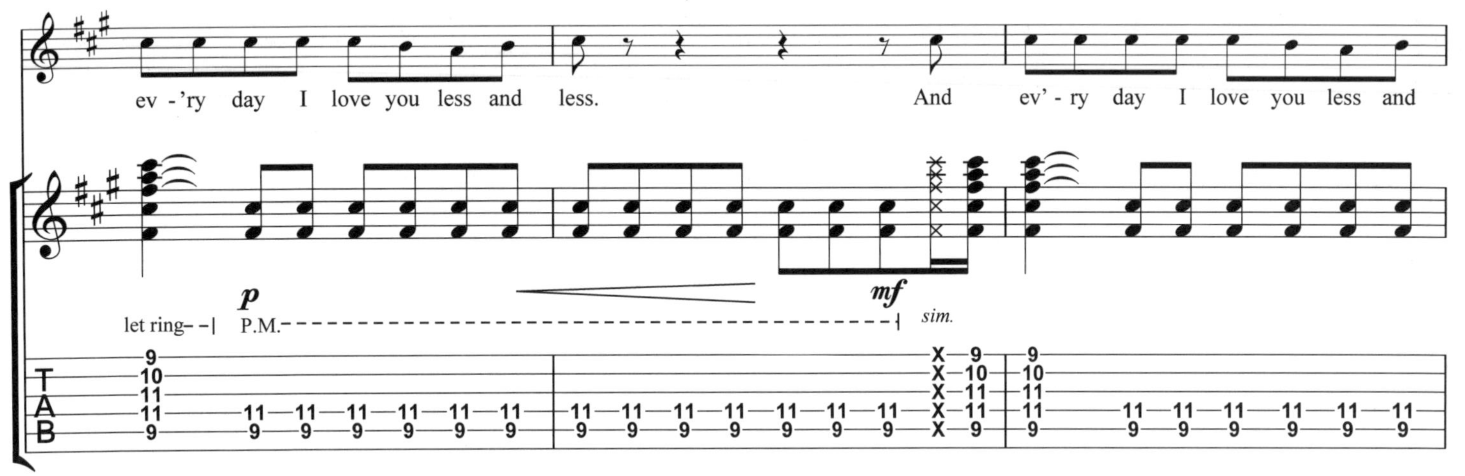
ev - 'ry day I love you less and less. And ev' - ry day I love you less and
let ring
P.M.
p
mf
sim.

less. I've got to get this feel - ing off my chest. The

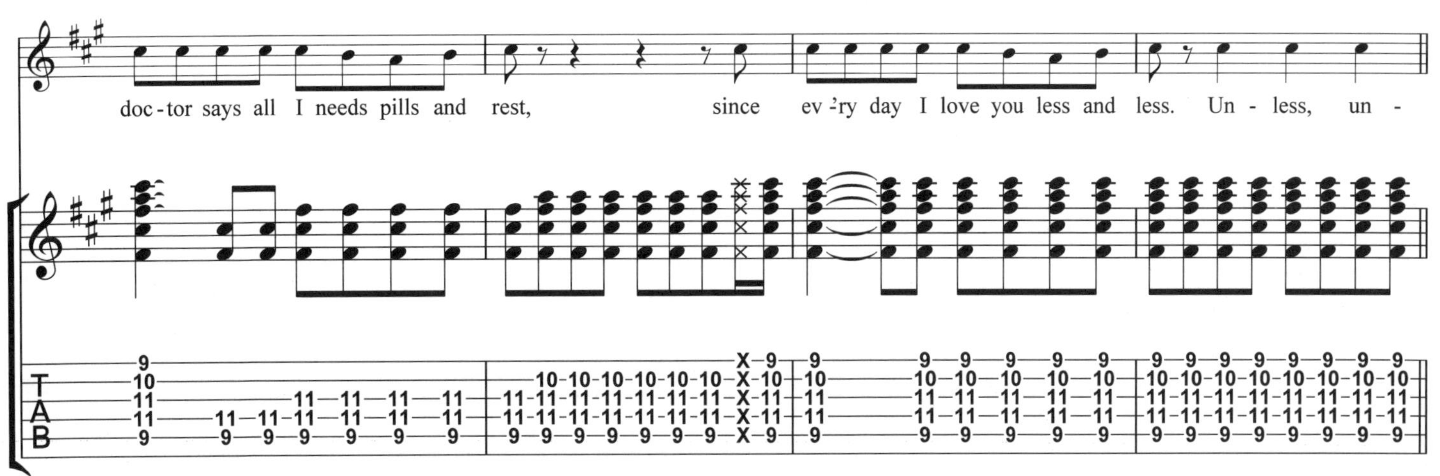
doc - tor says all I needs pills and rest, since ev -'ry day I love you less and less. Un - less, un -

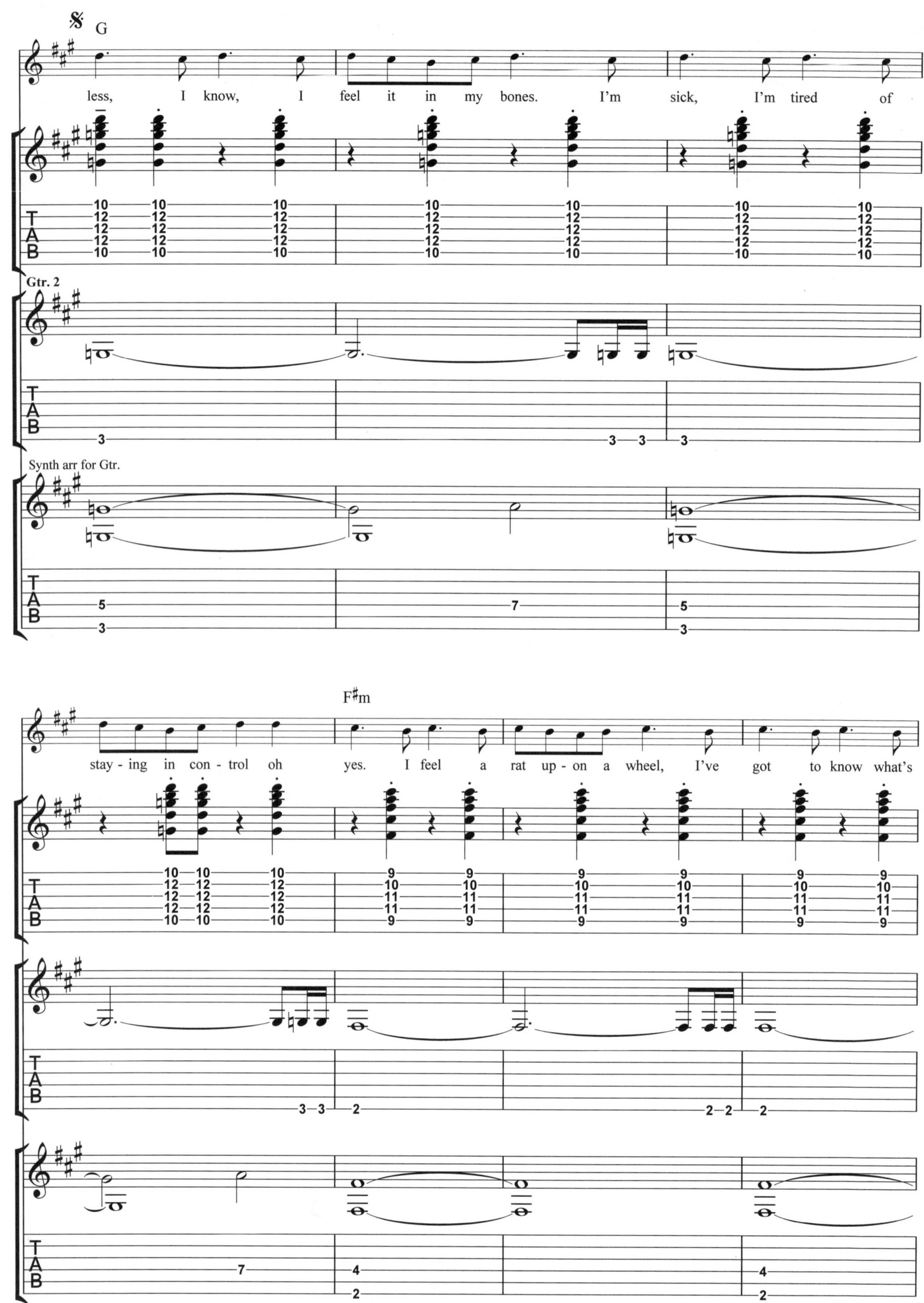
G
less, I know, I feel it in my bones. I'm sick, I'm tired of
Gtr. 2
Synth arr for Gtr.
F♯m
stay - ing in con - trol oh yes. I feel a rat up - on a wheel, I've got to know what's

G
not and what is real. Oh yes, I'm stressed, I'm sor - ry I dig-ressed. Im - pressed you're dressed to
Chorus
F♯5
E5
A5
S. - O. - S oh Oh oh, and my par - ents love me.
Gtr. 1 doubles Gtr. 2 until verse 2
P.M.

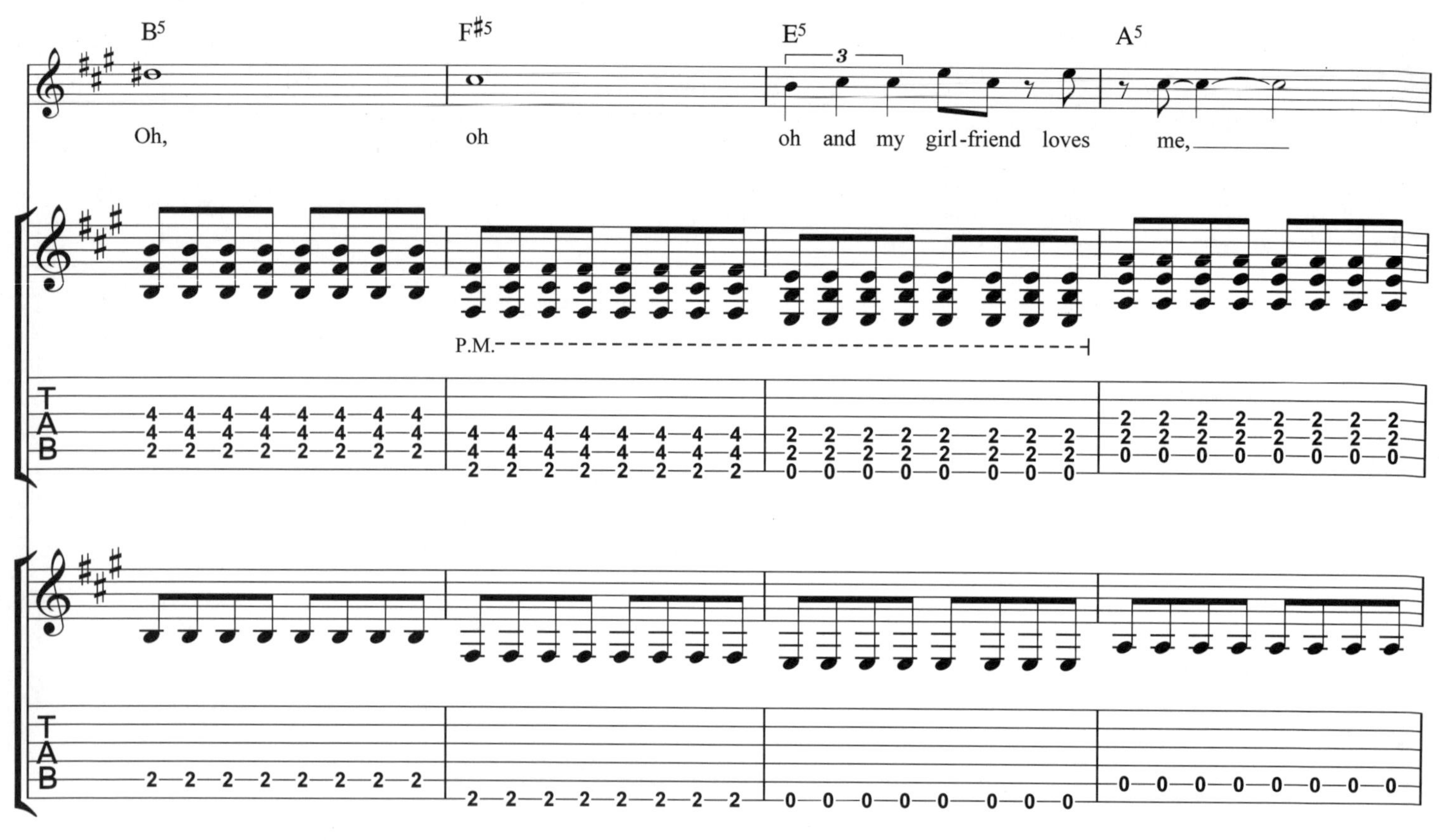
B5
F♯5
E5
A5
Oh,
oh
oh and my girl-friend loves me,
P.M.
T
A
B

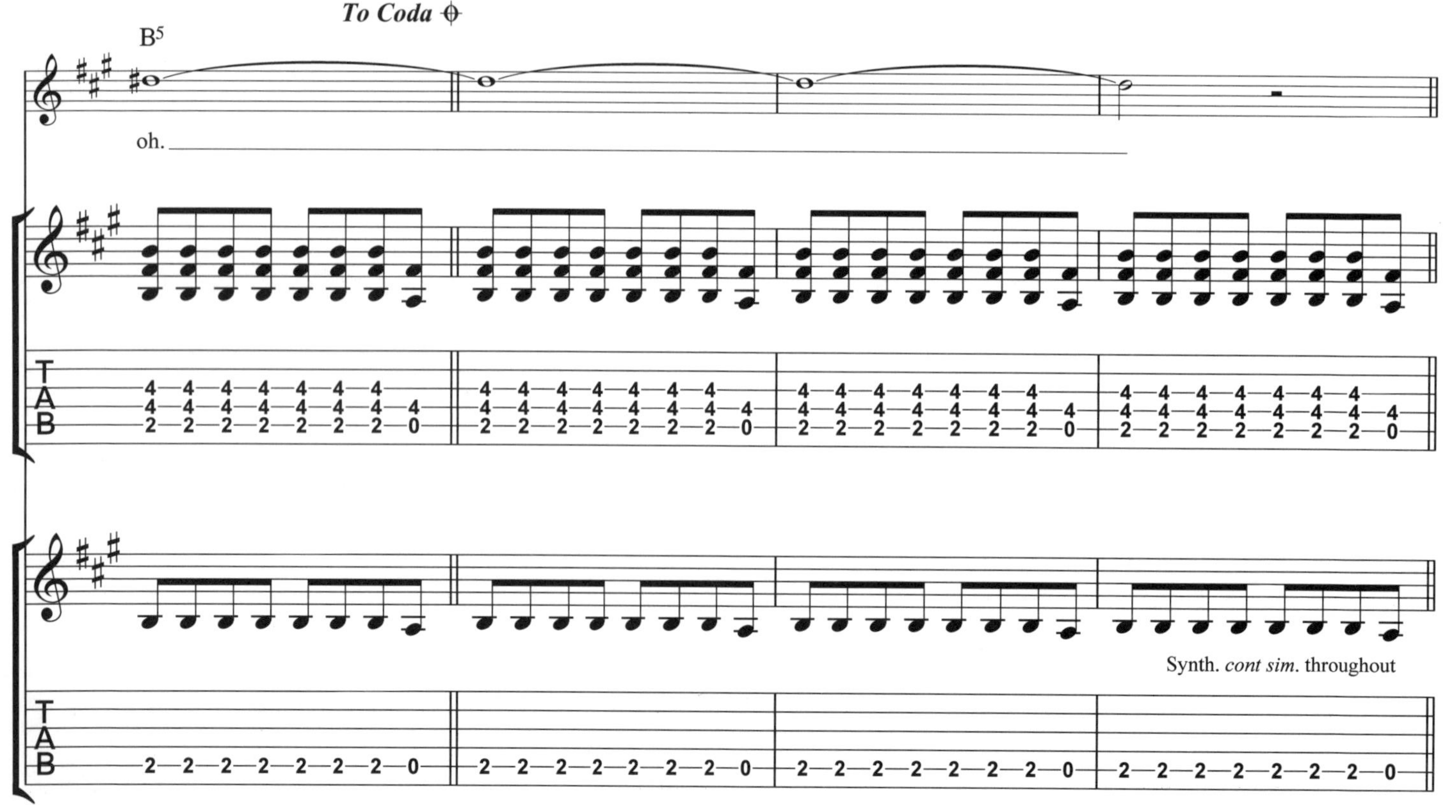
To Coda
B5
oh.
Synth. cont sim. throughout
T
A
B

Verse 2

F♯5
Ev - 'ry day I love you less and less. I can't be - lieve once you and me did
Gtr. 2
Synth. arr. for Gtr.

sex. Since ev - 'ry day I love you less and less, it makes me sick to think of you un-
Gtr. 1
Gtr. 2 as Verse 1
Synth. as Verse 1
let ring
P.M.

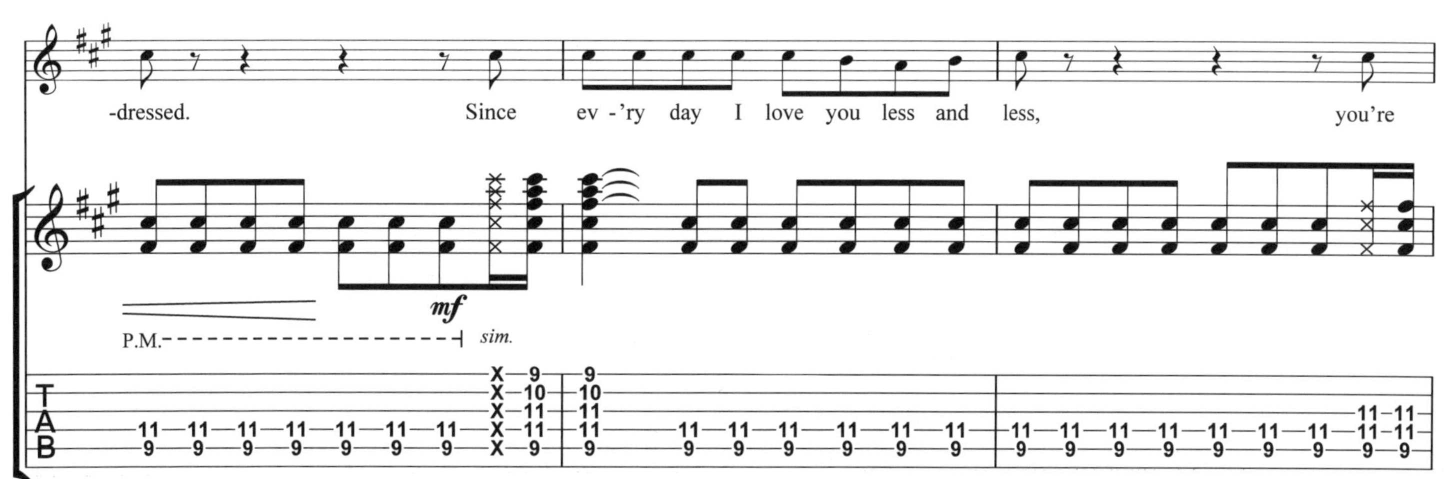
-dressed. Since ev - 'ry day I love you less and less, you're
P.M.
sim.

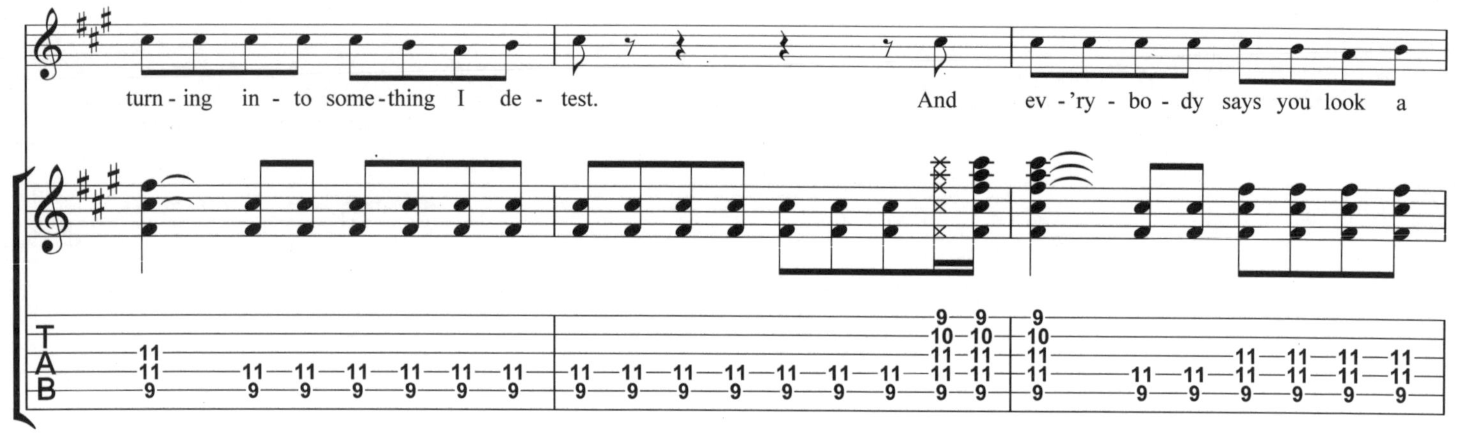
turn - ing in - to some - thing I de - test. And ev - 'ry - bo - dy says you look a

D.S. al Coda

mess, since eve - ry day I love you less and less and less.

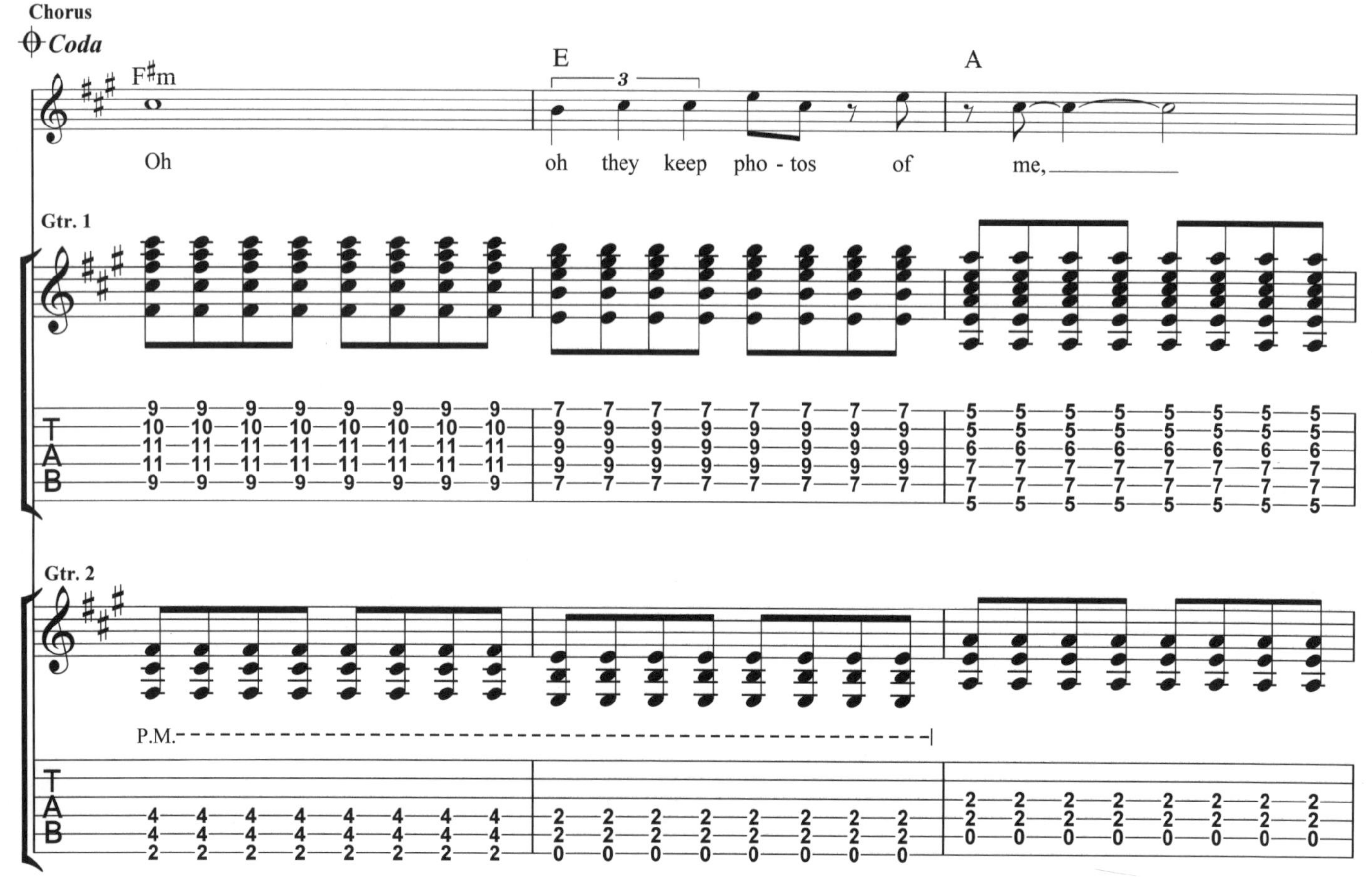
Chorus
Coda
F#m
E
A
Oh oh they keep pho - tos of me,
Gtr. 1
Gtr. 2
P.M.

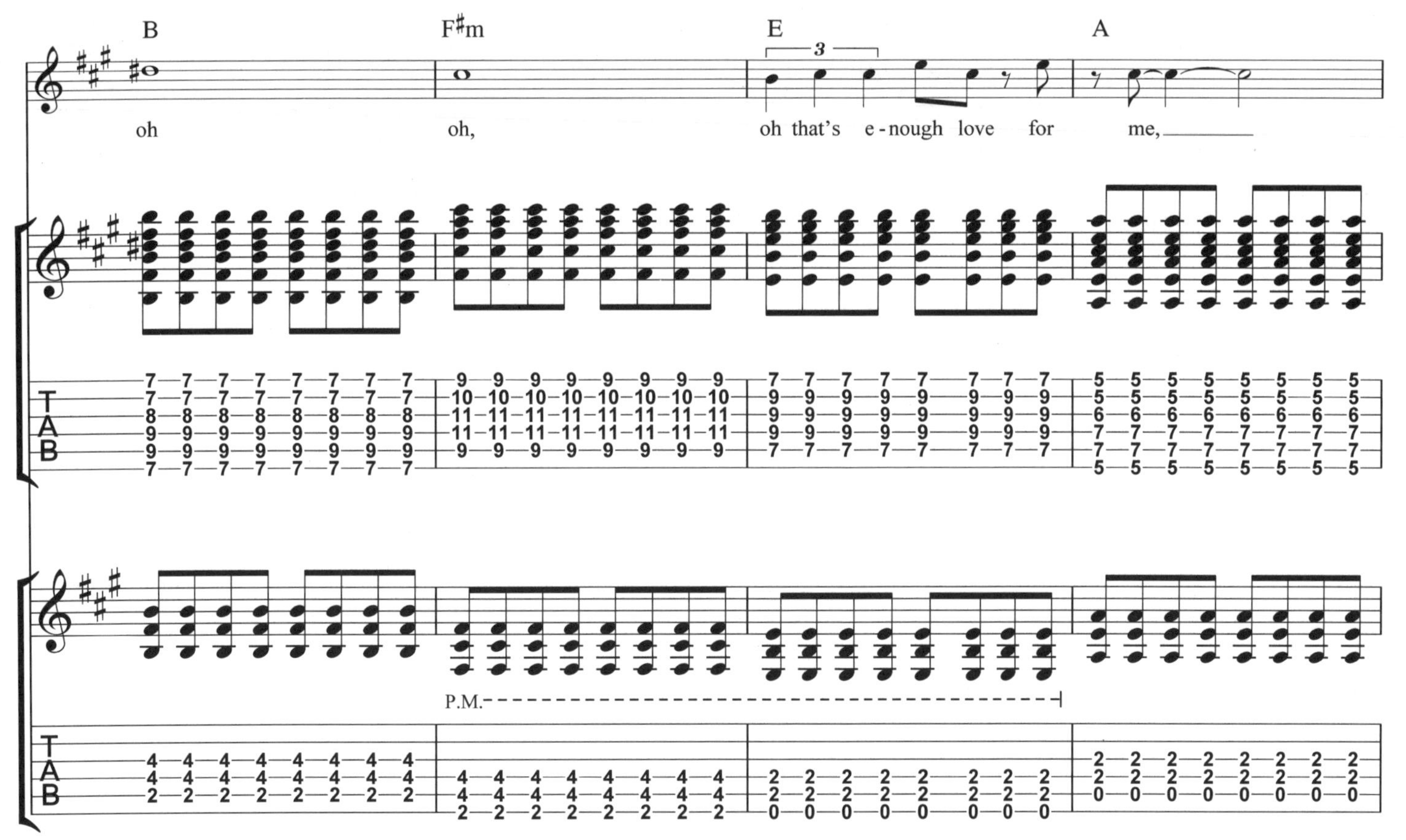
B
F♯m
E
A
oh
oh,
oh that's e - nough love for
me,
P.M.

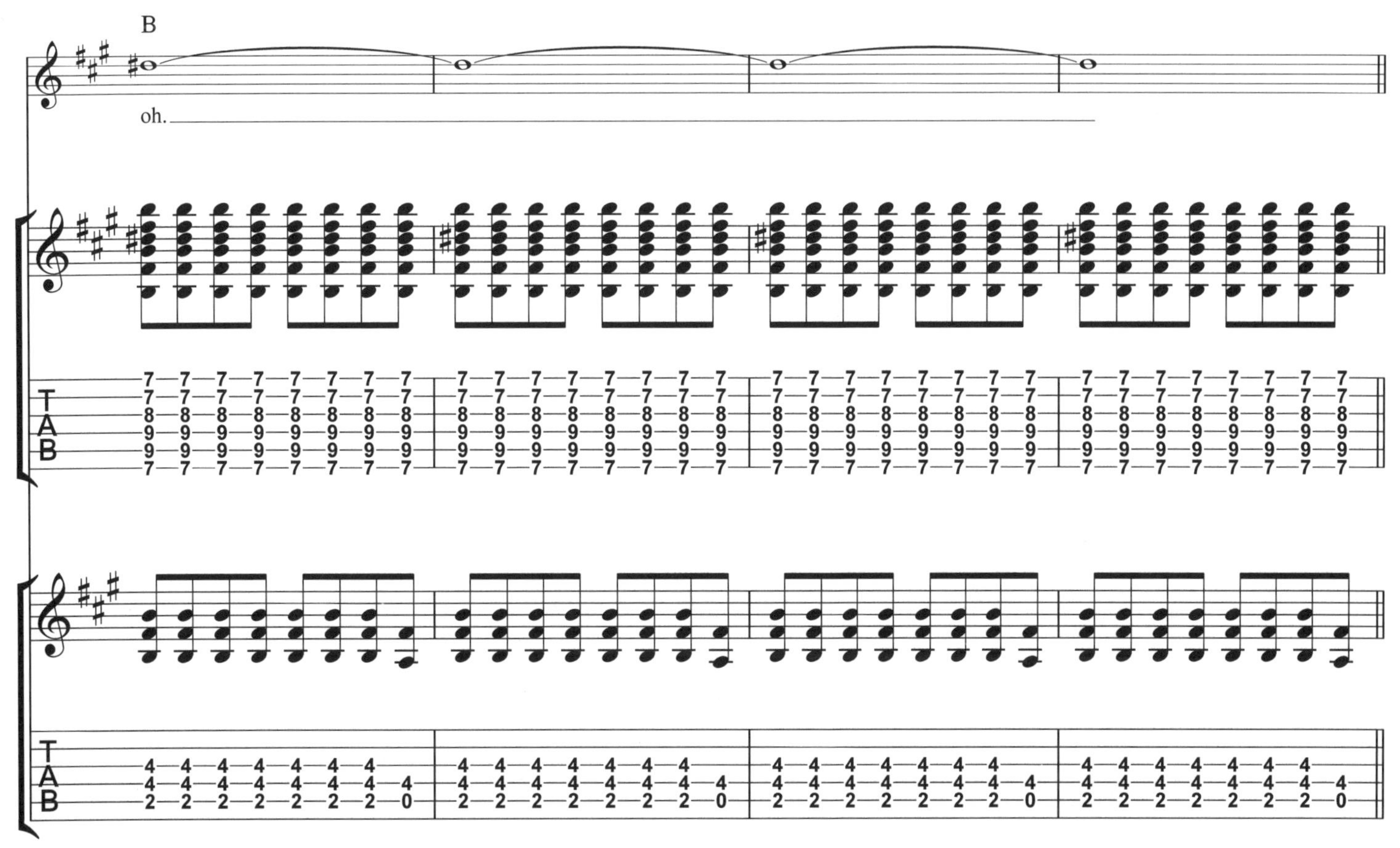
B
oh.

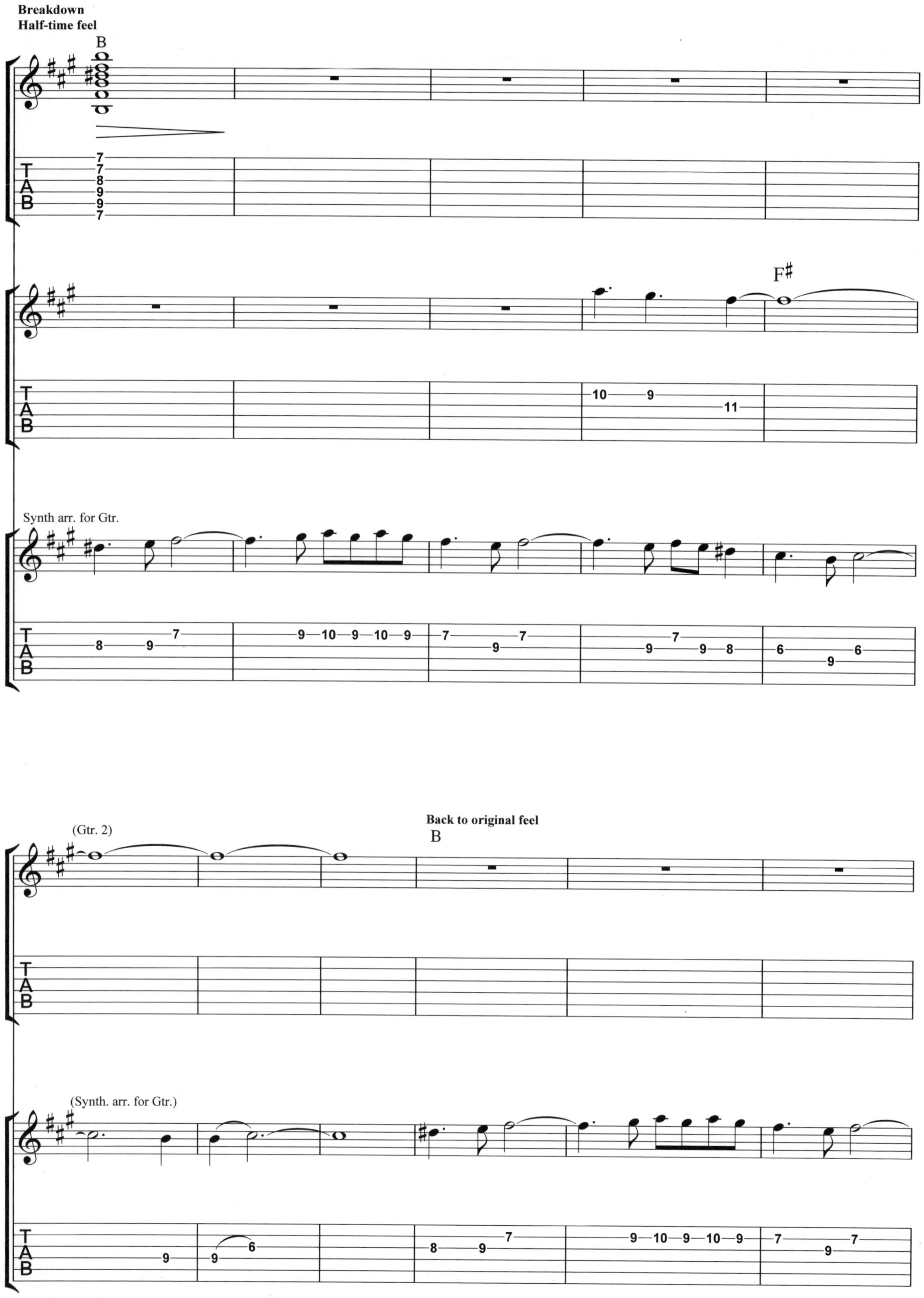

Breakdown
Half-time feel

B

F♯

Synth arr. for Gtr.

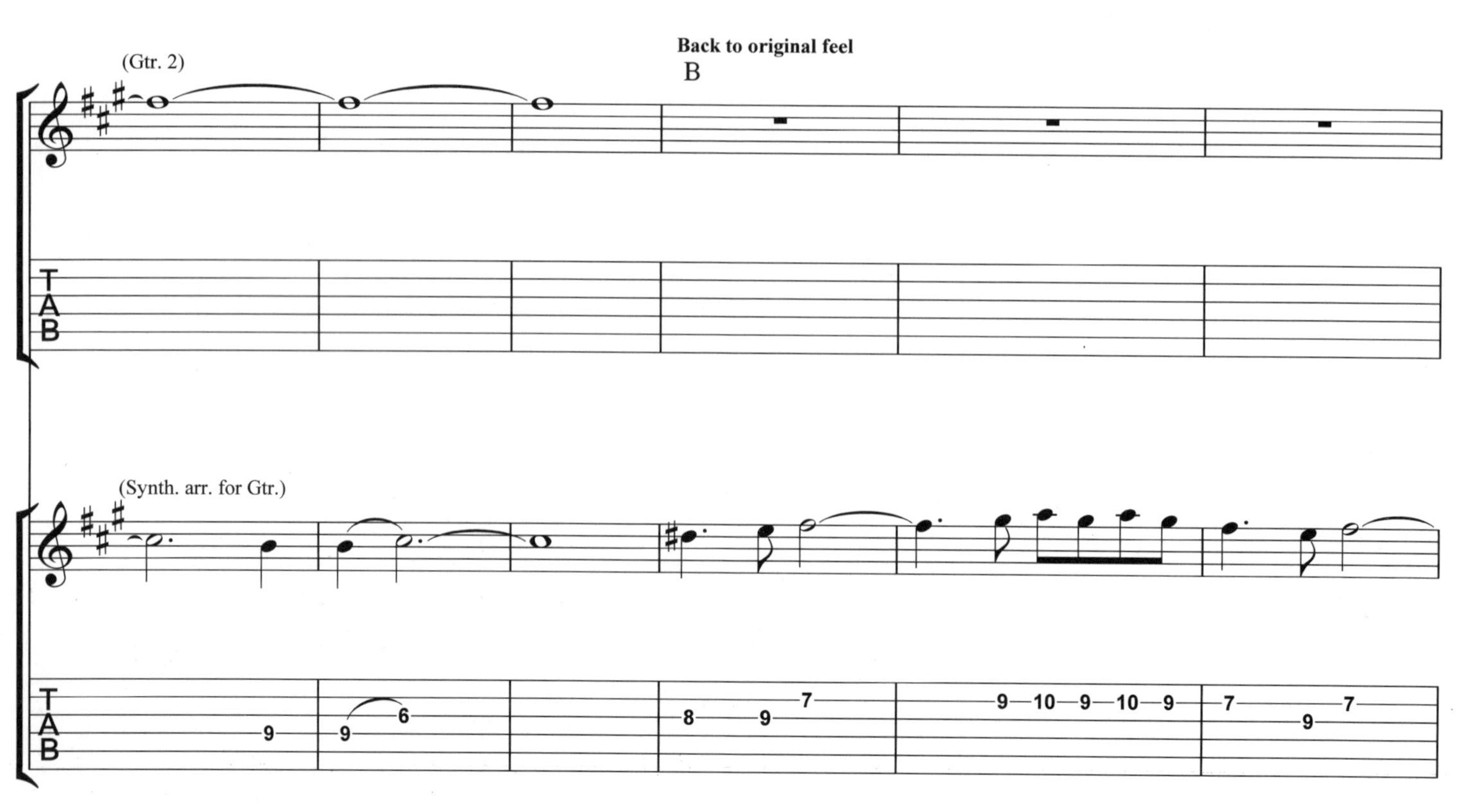

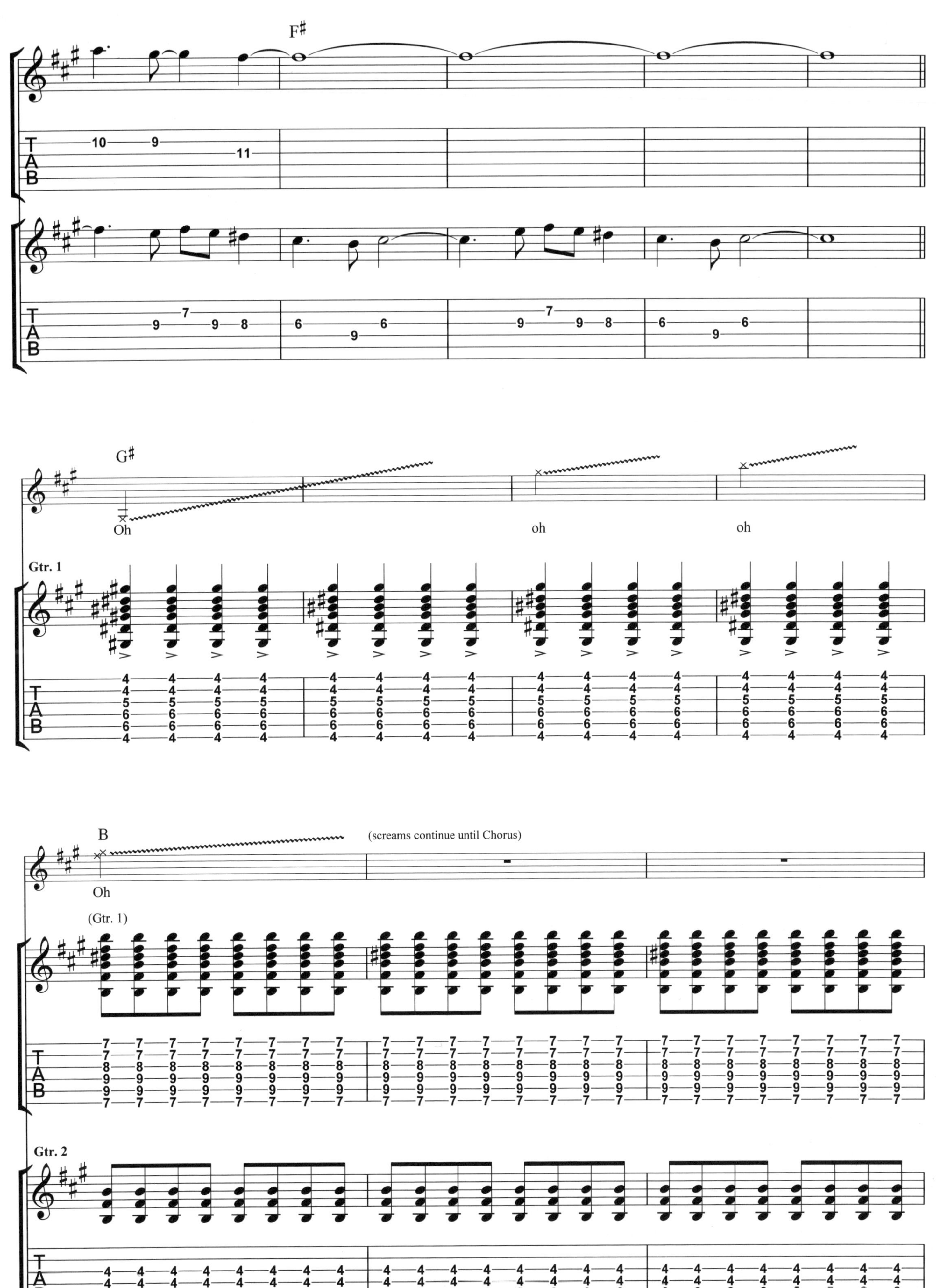
F♯
G♯
Oh
oh
oh
Gtr. 1
B
(screams continue until Chorus)
(Gtr. 1)
Gtr. 2

Chorus
F♯5
E5
Oh
oh and my par - ents love
P.M.
A5
B5
F♯5
E5
me.
Oh,
oh
oh and my girl-friend loves
P.M.
A5
B5
F♯m
E
me,
oh.
Oh
oh they keep pho - tos of
Gtr. 1
Gtr. 2 cont. sim.

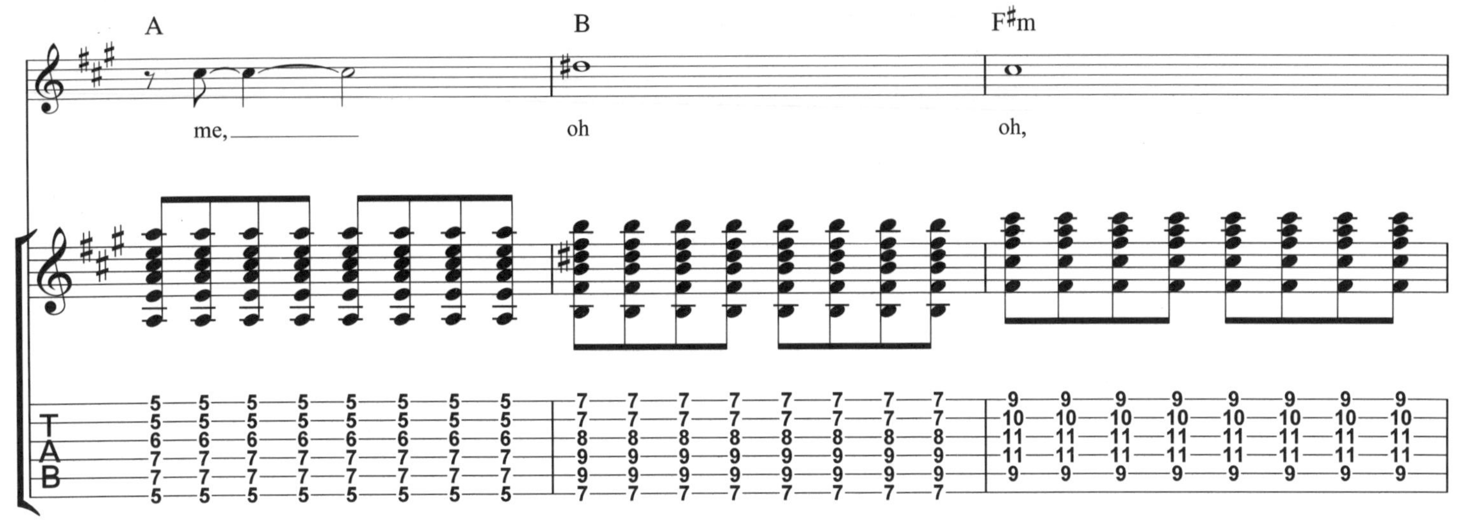
A
B
F#m
me,
oh
oh,

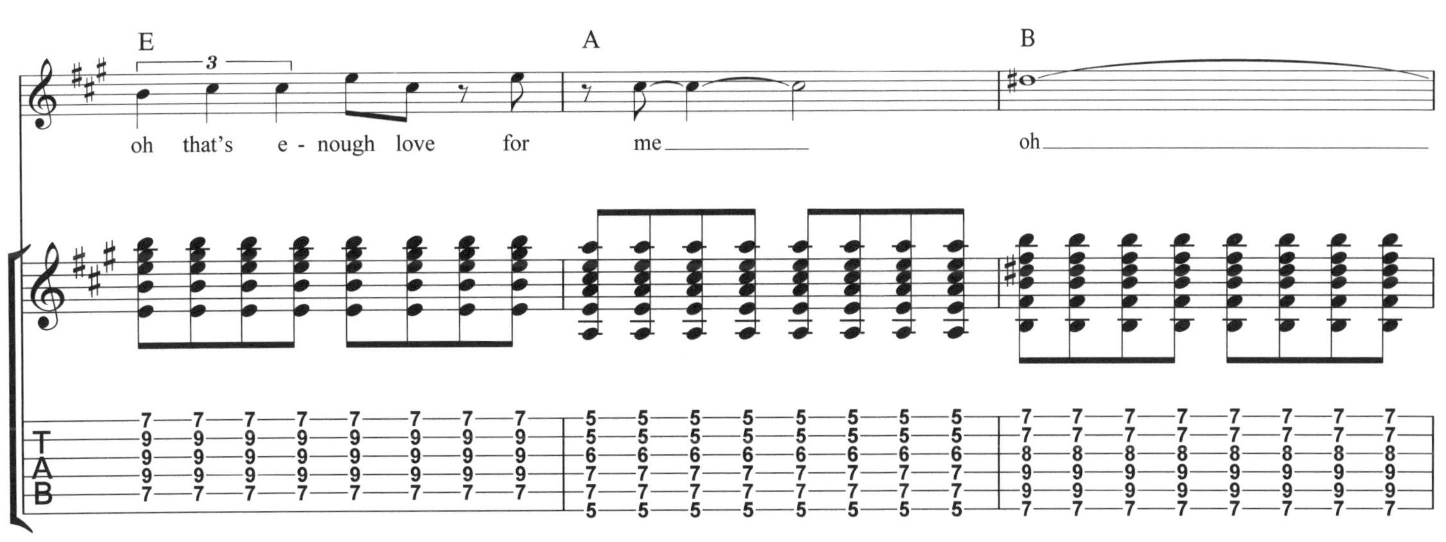
E
A
B
oh that's e - nough love for
me
oh

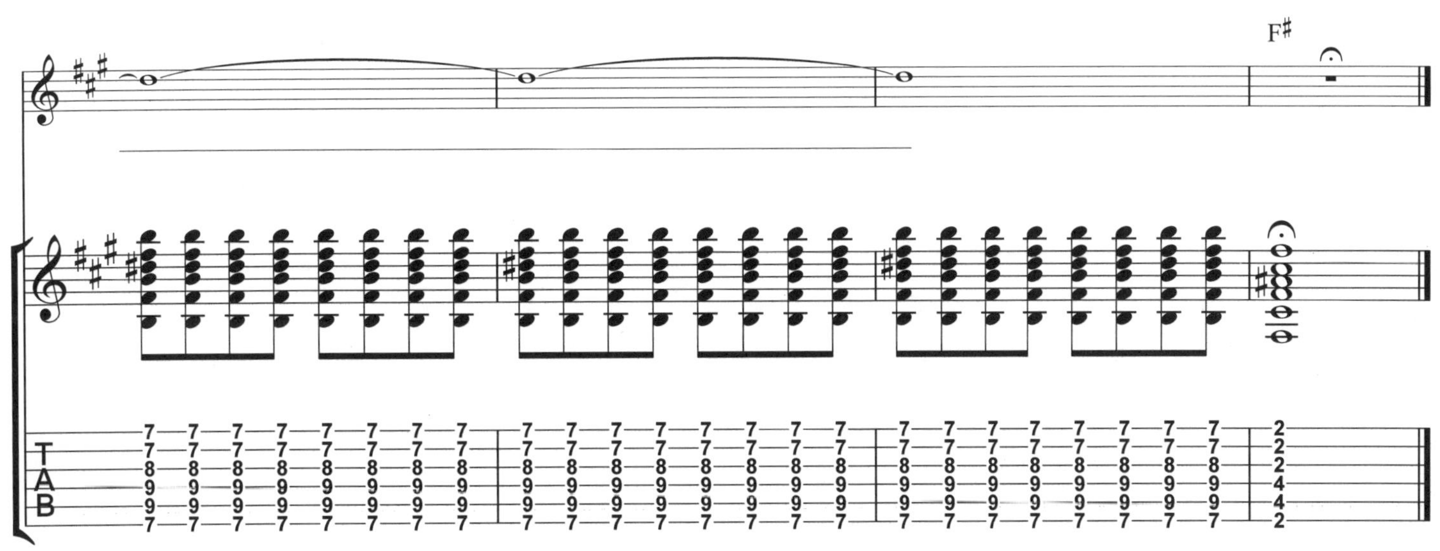
F#

I Predict A Riot

Words & Music by Nicholas Hodgson, Richard Wilson,
Andrew White, James Rix & Nicholas Baines

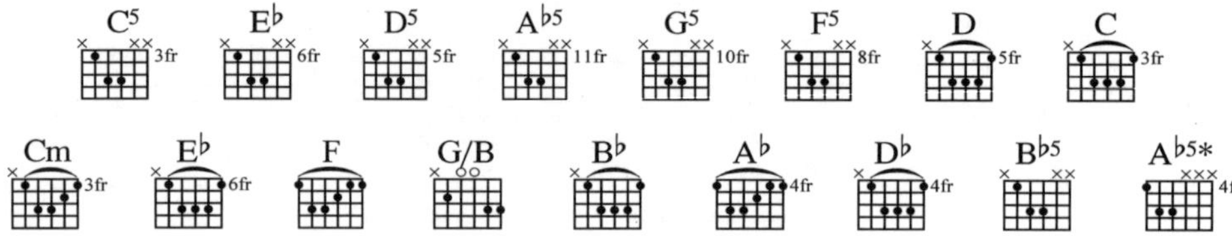

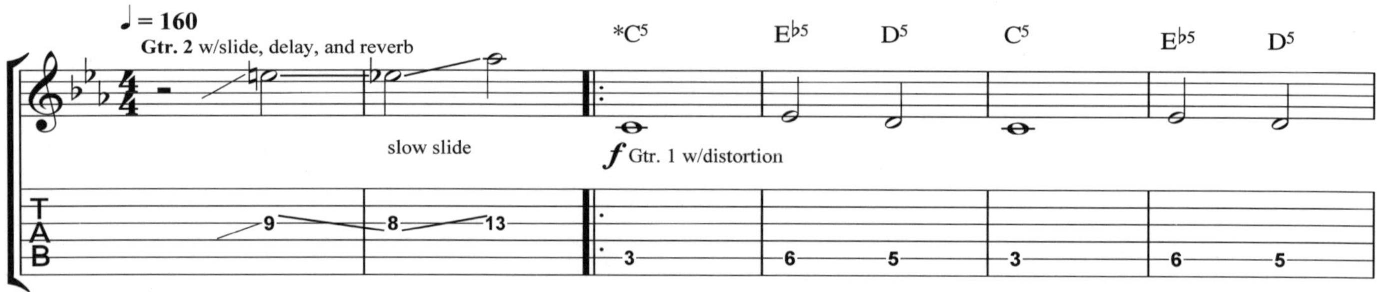

*Chords implied by harmony throughout except where indicated.

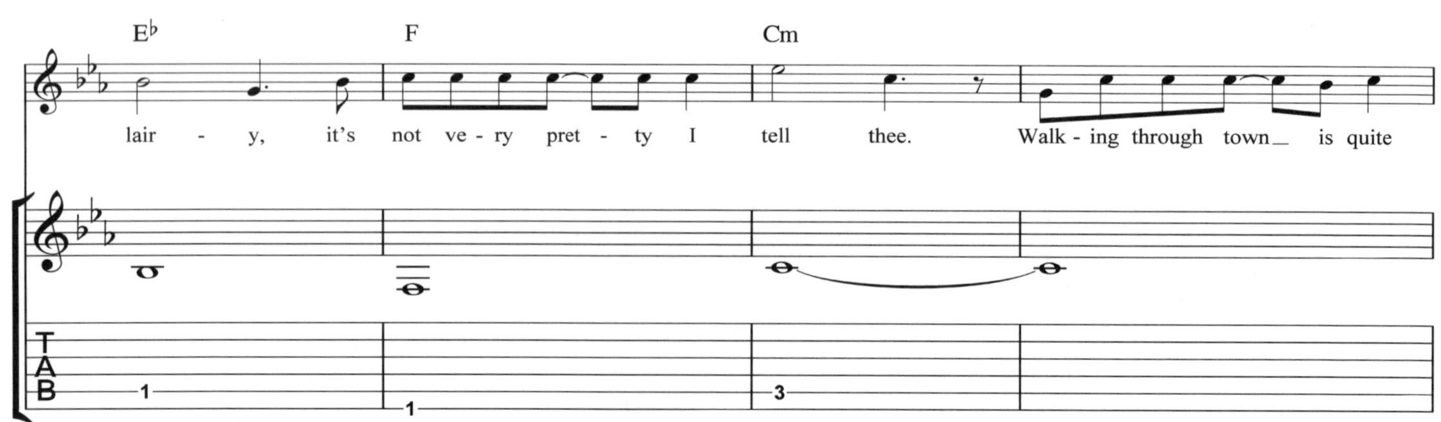

E♭
F
Cm
E♭
sca - ry, it's not ve-ry sen - si-ble eith - er. A friend of a friend he got beat - en, he
F
Cm
E♭
looked the wrong way at a pol - ice - man. Would ne-ver have happ - ened to Smea - ton, an
F
Pre-chorus
Cm
G/B
B♭
1.
F
2.
F
old Le-o-dens-i-an. Ah ah ah la la la la la la ah ah. la.
Chorus
A♭
D♭
A♭
I pre-dict a ri-ot. I pre-dict a ri-ot.

Verse
Cm
E♭
F
Cm
Oh, I tried to get to my ta - xi, the man in the track - suit at - tacks me. He
mf
said that he saw it be - fore me and wants things to get things a bit go - ry.
Girls scrab - ble round with no clothes on to bor - row a pound for a con - dom. If it
wa - n't for chip fat they'd be froz - en, they're not ve - ry sen - si - ble. Ah ah ah
Pre-chorus
G/B
TAB

B♭
1.
F
2.
F
Chorus
A♭
la la la la la la ah ah la.
I pre-dict a ri-ot.
f
D♭
A♭
Bridge
D5
(2° only)
I pre-dict a ri-ot.
And if there's an-y-bod-y left in
On D.S. only
(Tacet 1°)
C5
B♭5
To Coda
A♭5*
here that does-n't want to be out there.
oh
Guitar solo
C5
E♭5
D5
C5
E♭5
D5
Ah ah ah ah ah ah
Vocals 2° only
ff

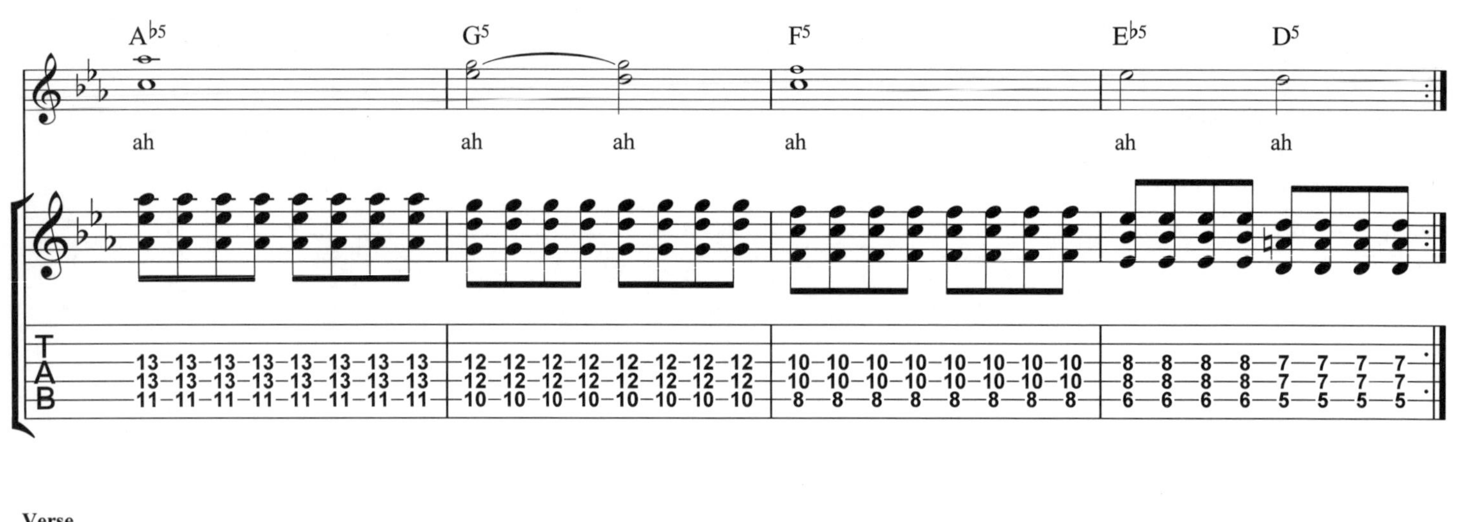
A♭5
G5
F5
E♭5
D5
ah
ah
ah
ah
ah
ah

Verse

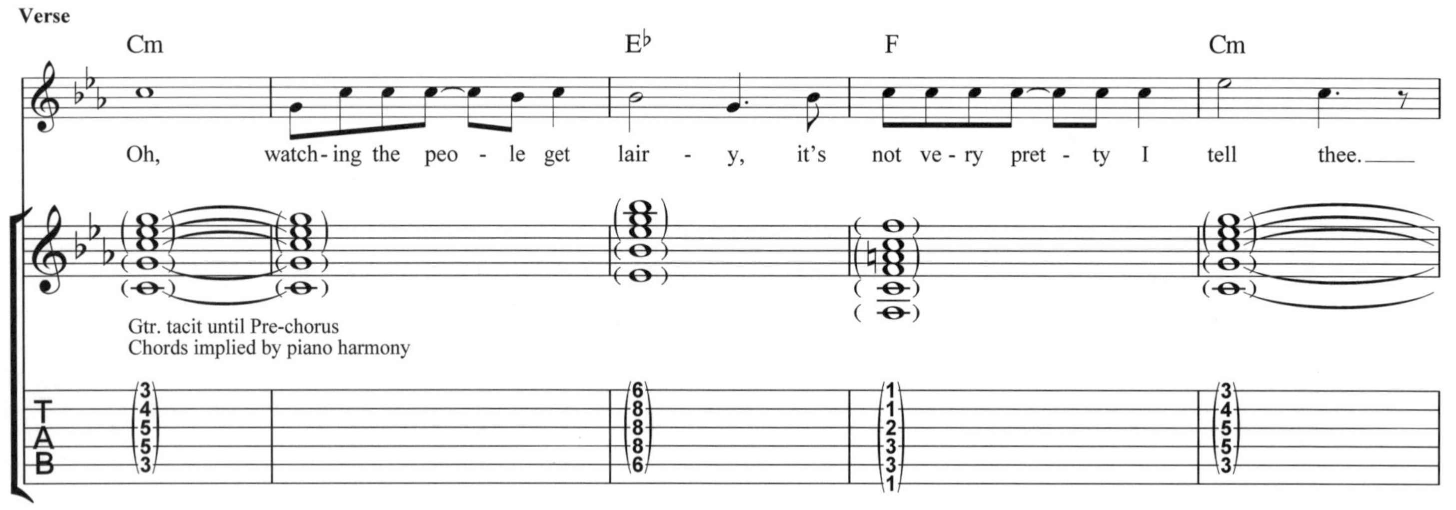
Cm
E♭
F
Cm
Oh, watch-ing the peo - le get lair - y, it's not ve-ry pret - ty I tell thee.
Gtr. tacit until Pre-chorus
Chords implied by piano harmony

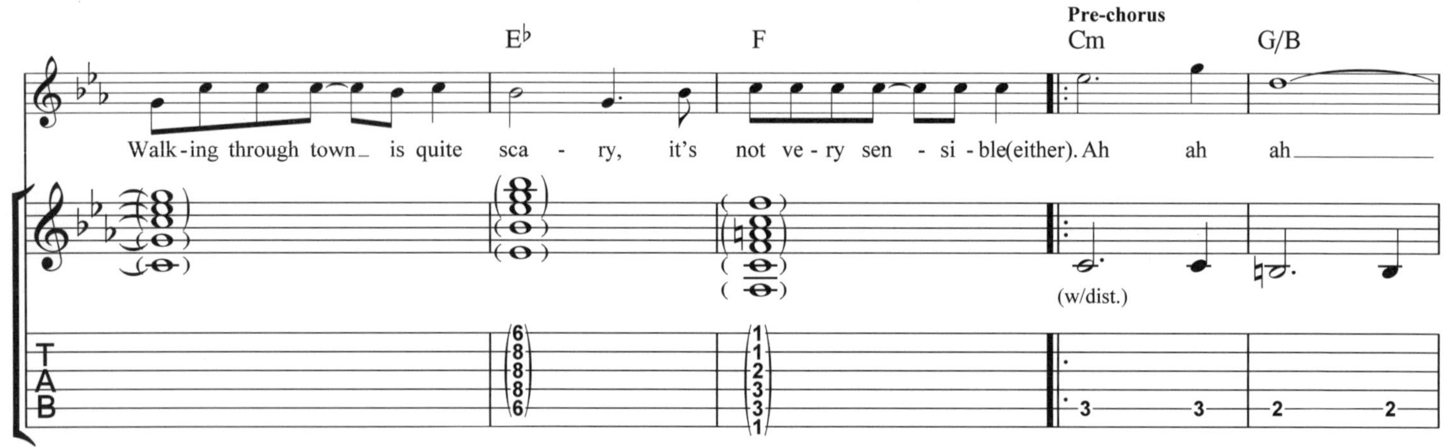
E♭
F
Pre-chorus
Cm
G/B
Walk-ing through town is quite sca - ry, it's not ve-ry sen - si - ble(either). Ah ah ah
(w/dist.)

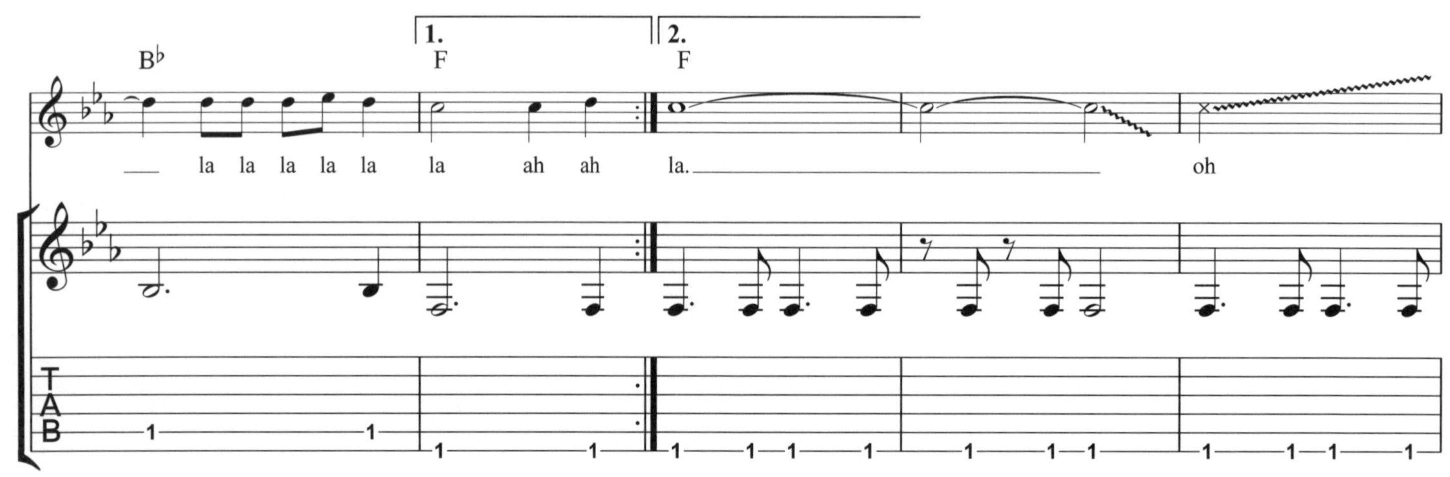
B♭
1.
F
2.
F
la la la la la la ah ah la. oh

D.S. al Coda
oh
oh
Coda
(A♭)
D♭
A♭
there. I pre - dict a ri - ot.
I pre - dict a ri - ot.
I pre - dict a ri - ot.
I pre - dict a ri - ot.
rubato, ad lib.
Gtr. 3 w/crunch tone

Modern Way

Words & Music by Nicholas Hodgson, Richard Wilson,
Andrew White, James Rix & Nicholas Baines

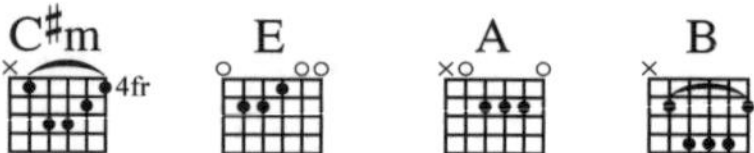

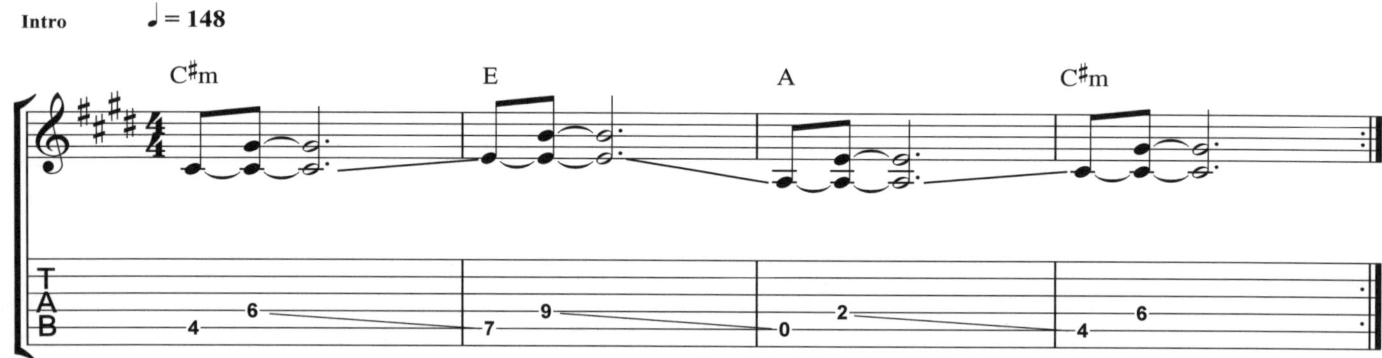

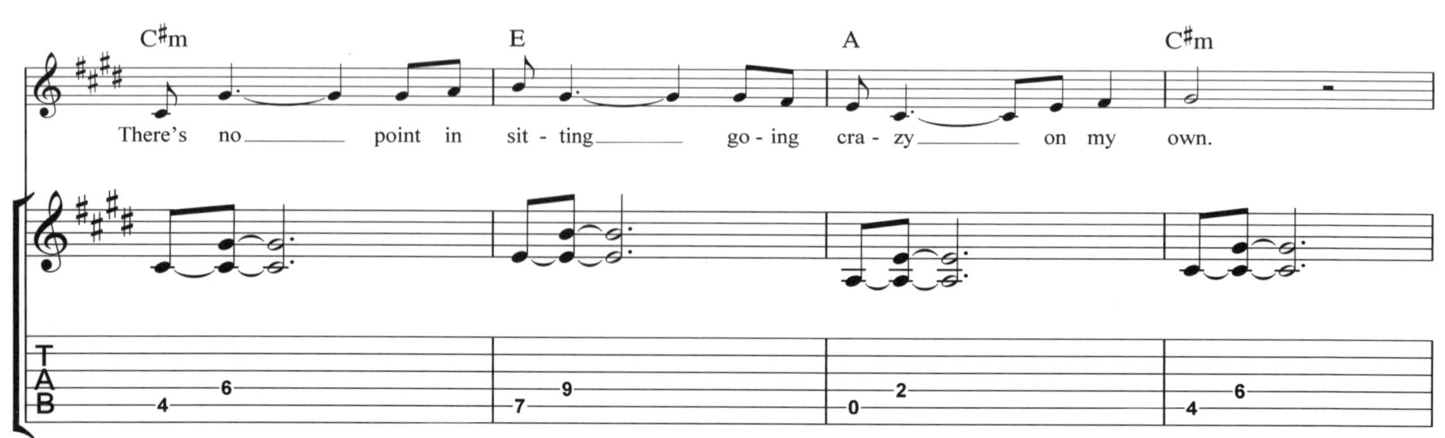

C♯m
E
A
C♯m
Do you know what I was put here in the world for.
Could you tell me in three words or more. It's the
Bridge
B
A
1° only
on - ly way of get - ting out of here It's the
Ah
Ah
cont. sim.
Verse
Take a les - son from the ones who have been there.

C♯m E A C♯m
My brain is not dam - aged but in need of some re - pair.
C♯m E A C♯m
Hold on to the bas - ics but we can change all our tac - tics.
C♯m E A C♯m
There's no point in sit - ting go - ing cra - zy on your own. It's the
Bridge
B A
on - ly way of get - ting out of here It's the
Ah
Ah
cont. sim.

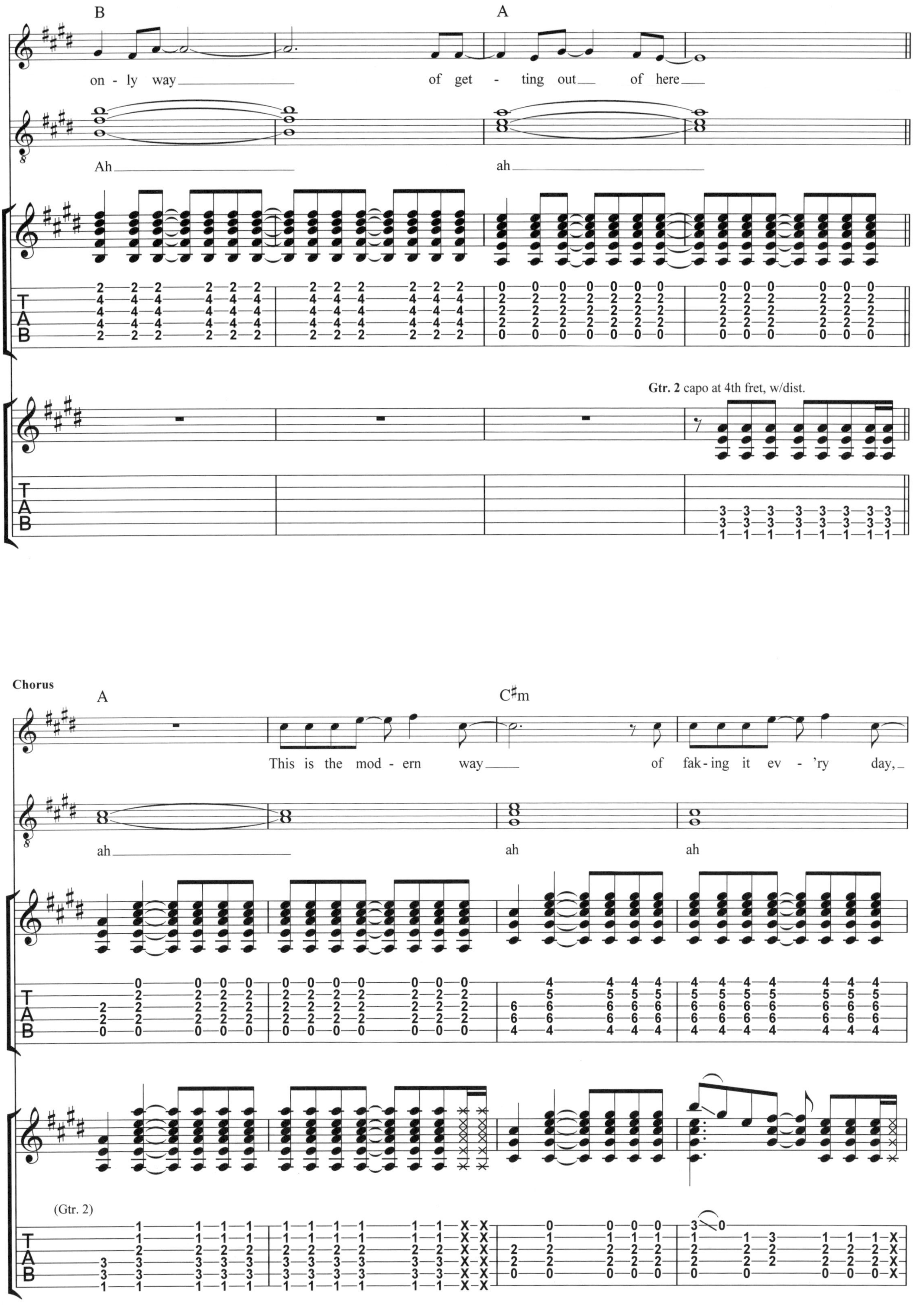

B A

on - ly way of get - ting out of here

Ah ah

Gtr. 2 capo at 4th fret, w/dist.

Chorus

A C♯m

This is the mod - ern way of fak - ing it ev - 'ry day,

ah ah ah

(Gtr. 2)

A C♯m

and tak-ing it as we come. And we're not the on-ly ones.

ah ah ah

A C♯m

Is that what we used to say. This is the mod-ern way

ah ah ah

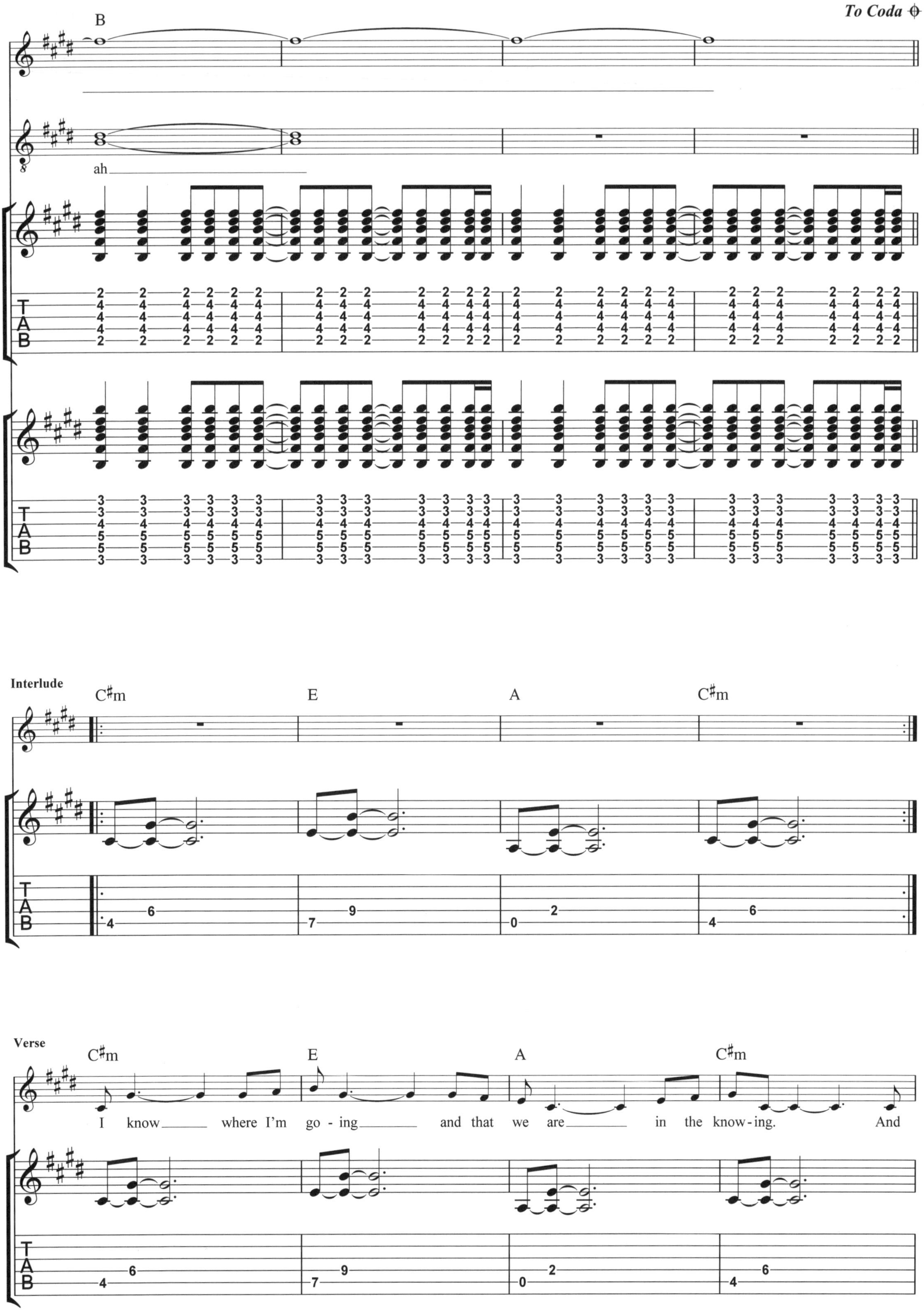

To Coda ⊕

B

ah

Interlude

Verse

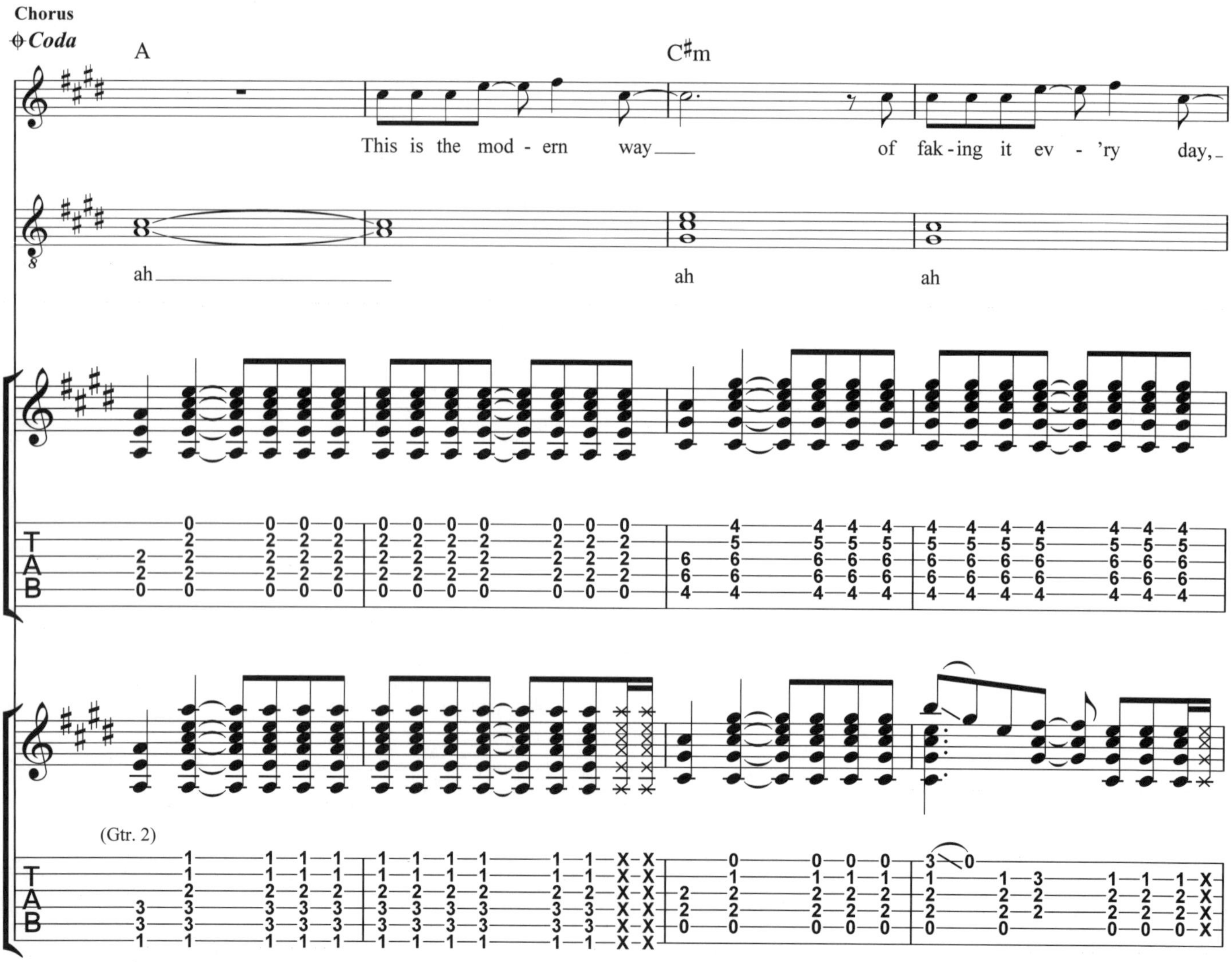

Chorus

Coda

A C♯m

This is the mod - ern way of fak - ing it ev - 'ry day,

ah ah ah

(Gtr. 2)

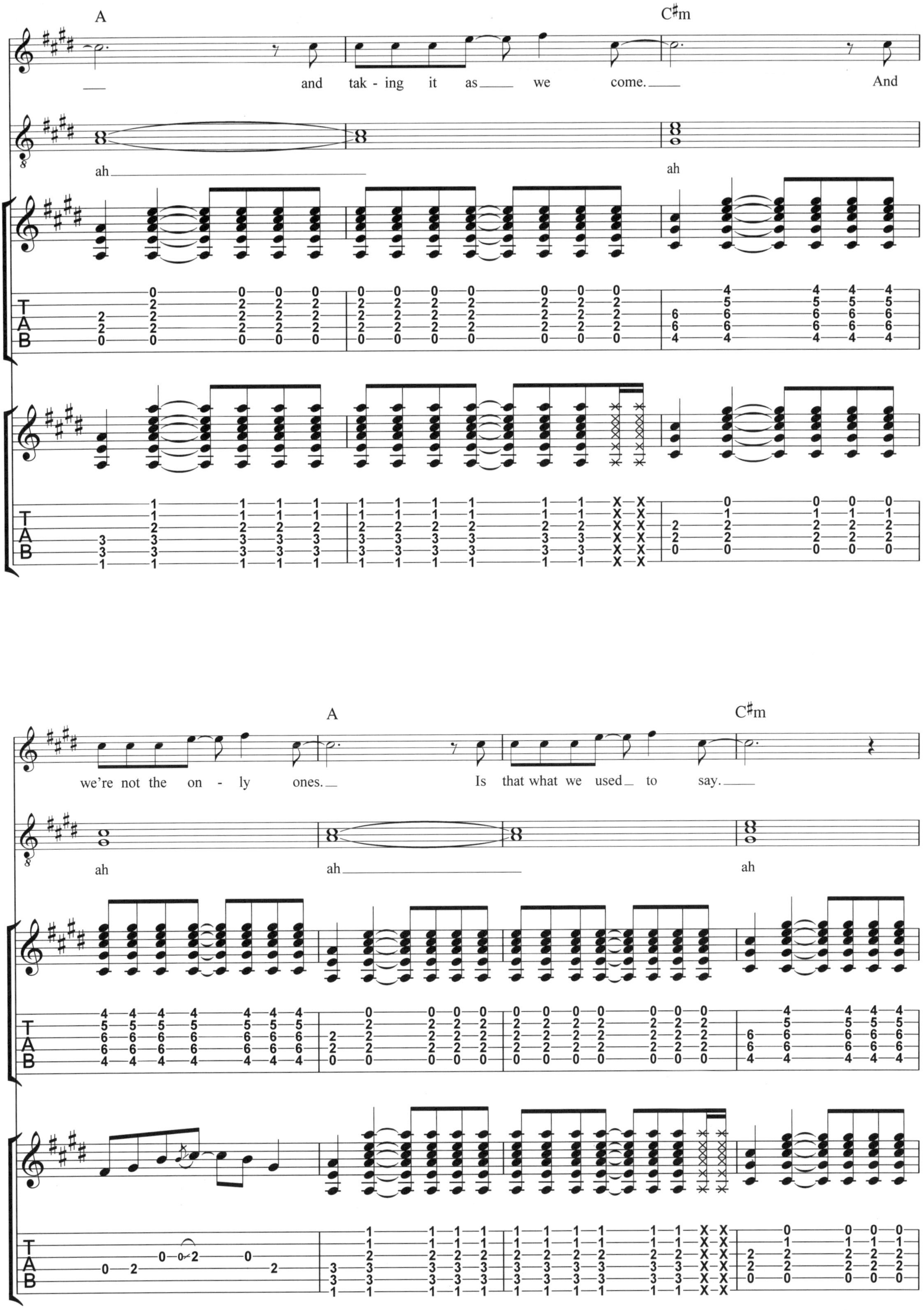

A C♯m

and tak - ing it as we come. And

ah ah

A C♯m

we're not the on - ly ones. Is that what we used to say.

ah ah ah

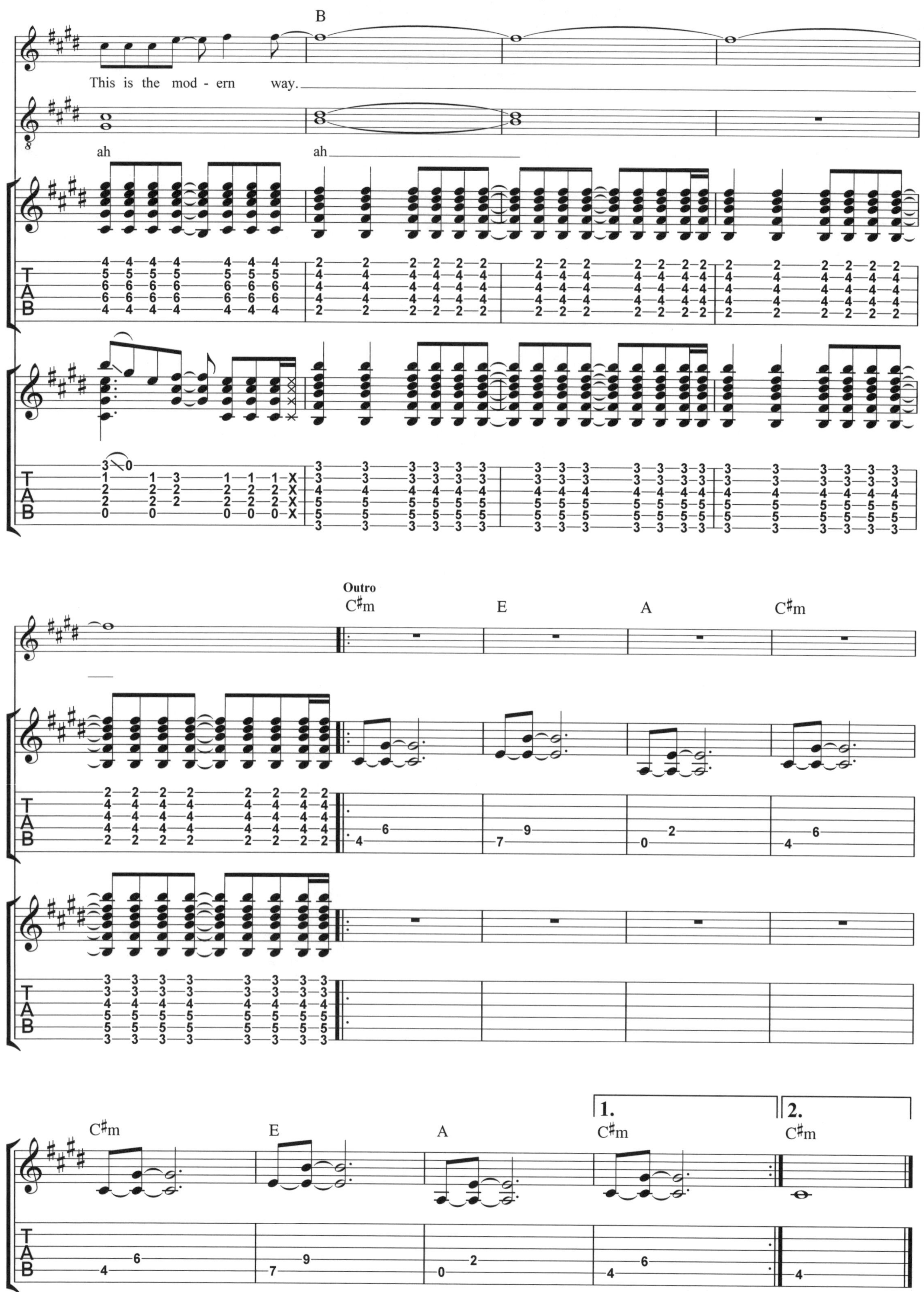
B
This is the mod - ern way.
ah
ah
Outro
C♯m
E
A
C♯m
C♯m
E
A
1.
C♯m
2.
C♯m

Na Na Na Na Naa

Words & Music by Nicholas Hodgson, Richard Wilson,
Andrew White, James Rix & Nicholas Baines

E
A
B

♩ = 160
1 2 1 2 3 4
E
Na na na na naa.
Keyboard arr. for Gtr.

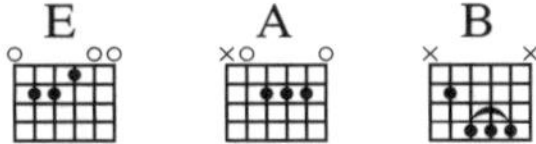

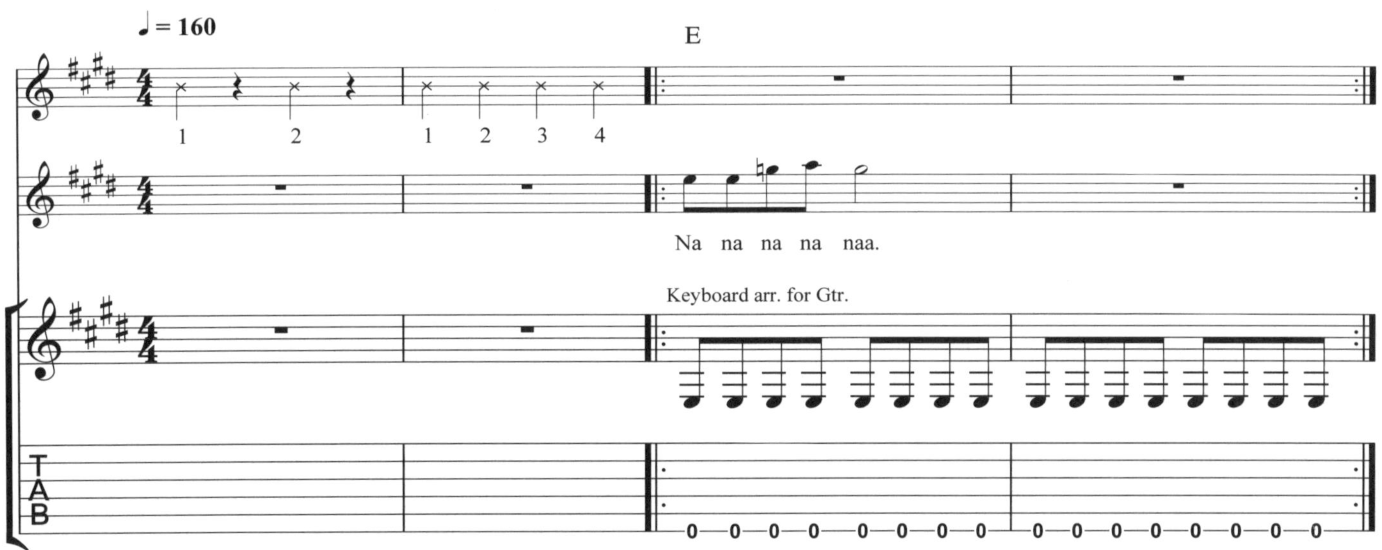

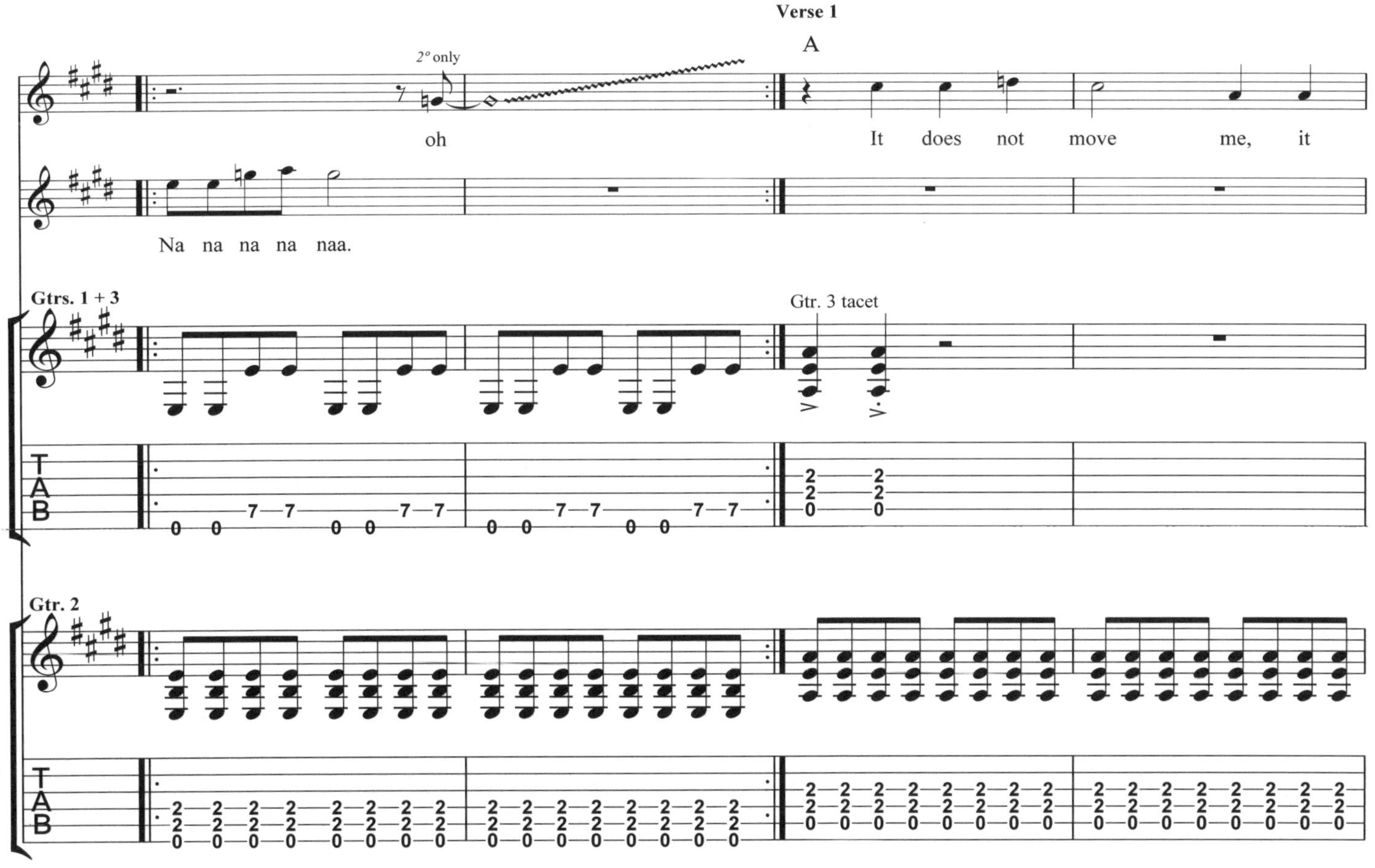

Verse 1
A
2° only
oh
It does not move me, it
Na na na na naa.
Gtrs. 1 + 3
Gtr. 3 tacet
Gtr. 2

E

does not get me go - ing at all.

Na na na na naa.

Gtrs. 1 + 3

T
A
B
0—0—7—7—0—0—7—7—0—0—7—7—0—0—7—7

2—2—2—2—2—2—2—2—2—2—2—2—2—2—2—2—2—2—2—2—2—2—2—2—2—2—2—2—2—2—2—2
2—2—2—2—2—2—2—2—2—2—2—2—2—2—2—2—2—2—2—2—2—2—2—2—2—2—2—2—2—2—2—2
0—0—0—0—0—0—0—0—0—0—0—0—0—0—0—0—0—0—0—0—0—0—0—0—0—0—0—0—0—0—0—0

A

It does not shift me, it's not the kind of thing that I like.

Gtr. 3 tacet

2 2
2 2
0 0

2—2—2—2—2—2—2—2—2—2—2—2—2—2—2—2—2—2—2—2—2—2—2—2—2—2—2—2—2—2—2—2
2—2—2—2—2—2—2—2—2—2—2—2—2—2—2—2—2—2—2—2—2—2—2—2—2—2—2—2—2—2—2—2
0—0—0—0—0—0—0—0—0—0—0—0—0—0—0—0—0—0—0—0—0—0—0—0—0—0—0—0—0—0—0—0

E

B

It does not move me, it's

Na na na na naa

Gtrs. 1 + 3

Gtr. 3 tacet

A

E

not the kind of thing that I like.

Na na na na naa.

Gtrs. 1 + 3

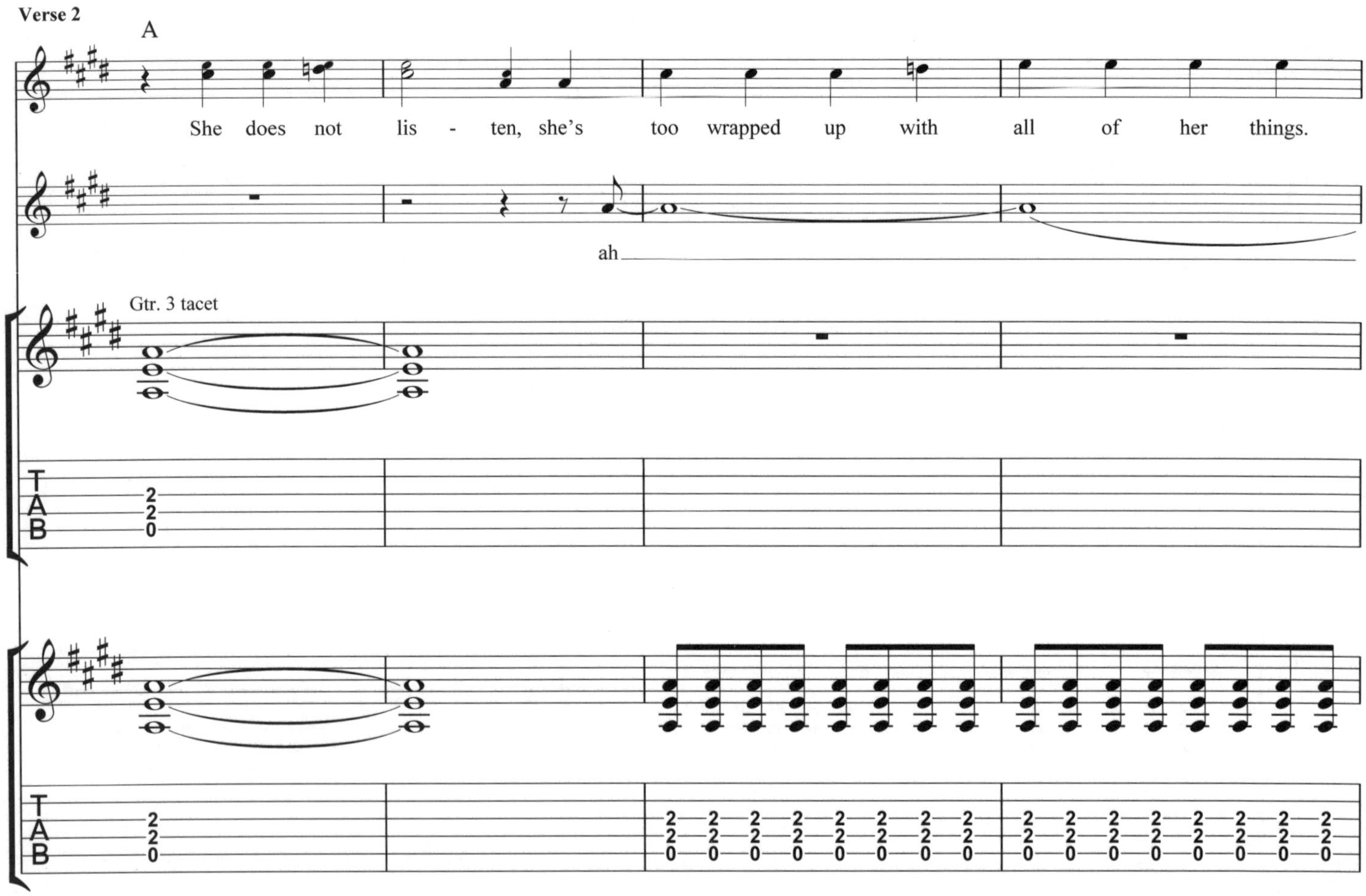
Verse 2
A
She does not lis - ten, she's too wrapped up with all of her things.
ah
Gtr. 3 tacet
TAB

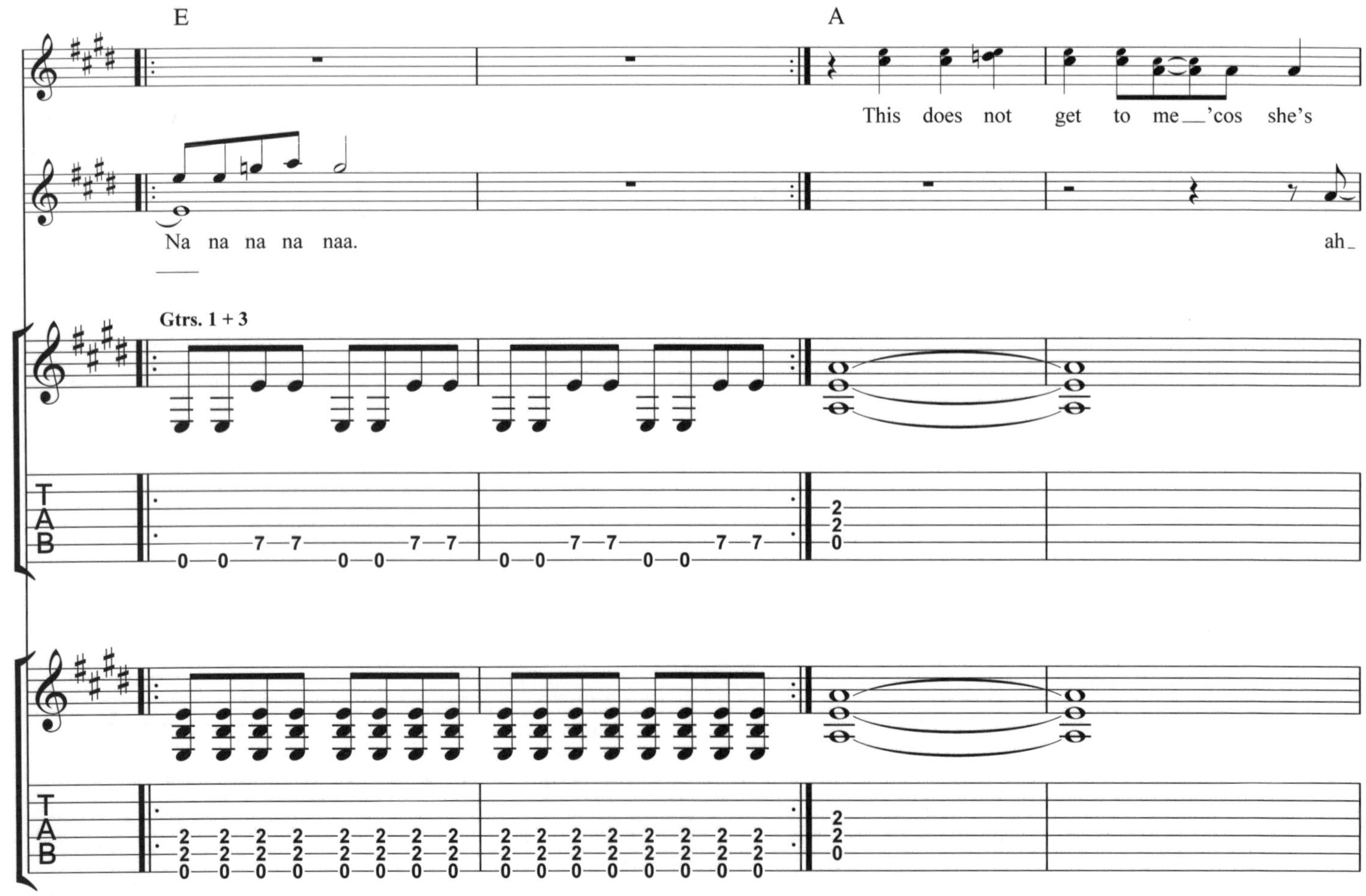
E
A
This does not get to me 'cos she's
Na na na na naa.
ah
Gtrs. 1 + 3
TAB

E
2° only
not the kind of girl that I like
oh.
Na na na na naa.
Gtrs 1 + 3
B
A
She does not move me, she's not the kind of girl that I like.

E
Oh.
Na na na na naa.
Na na na na naa.
Gtrs. 1 + 3
Gtr. 3 tacet
HO
Guitar solo
full
hold bend

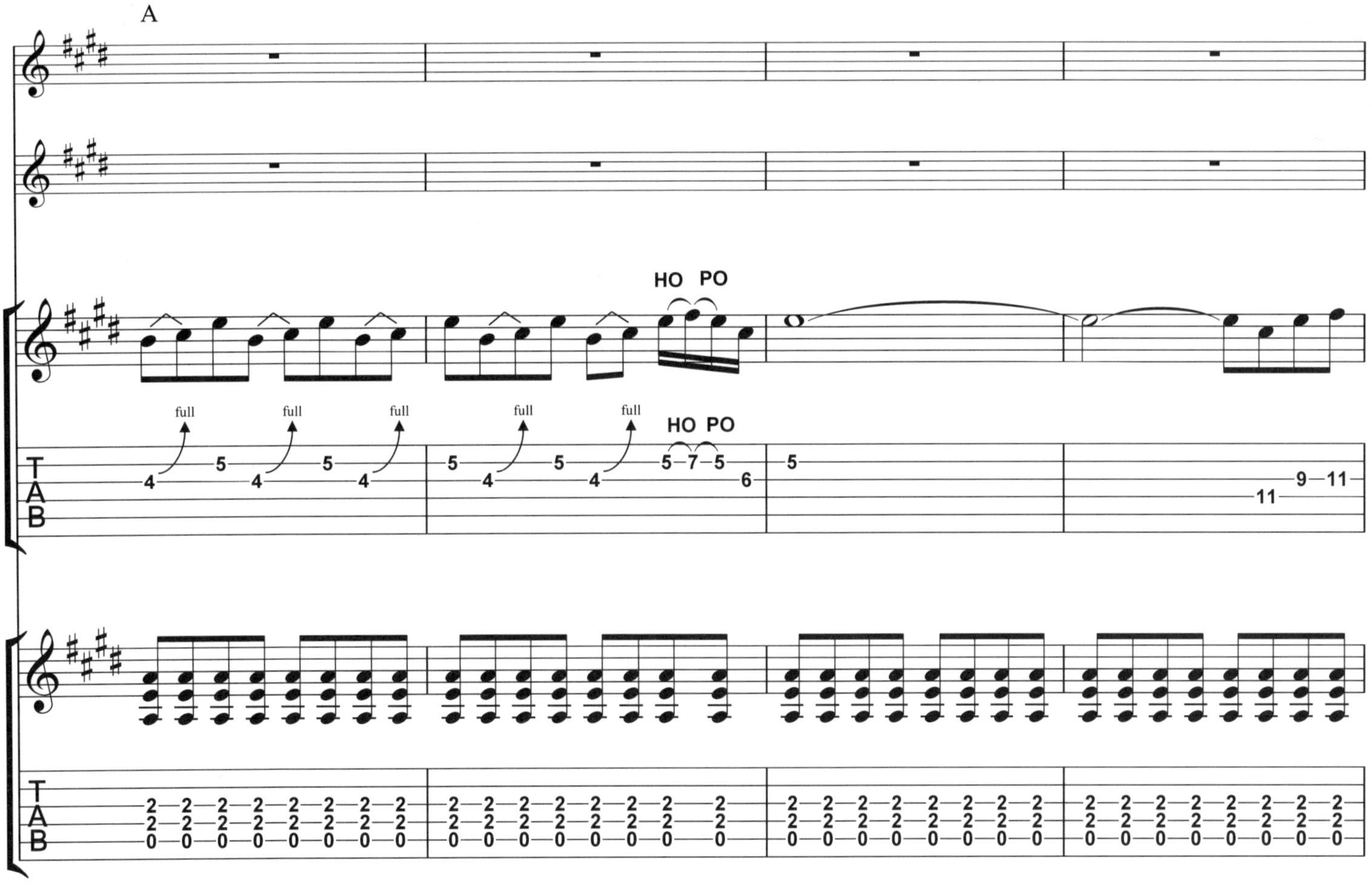
A
HO PO
full
full
full
full
full
HO PO

E
Oh.
full
full
full
full
full
full
pick scrapes

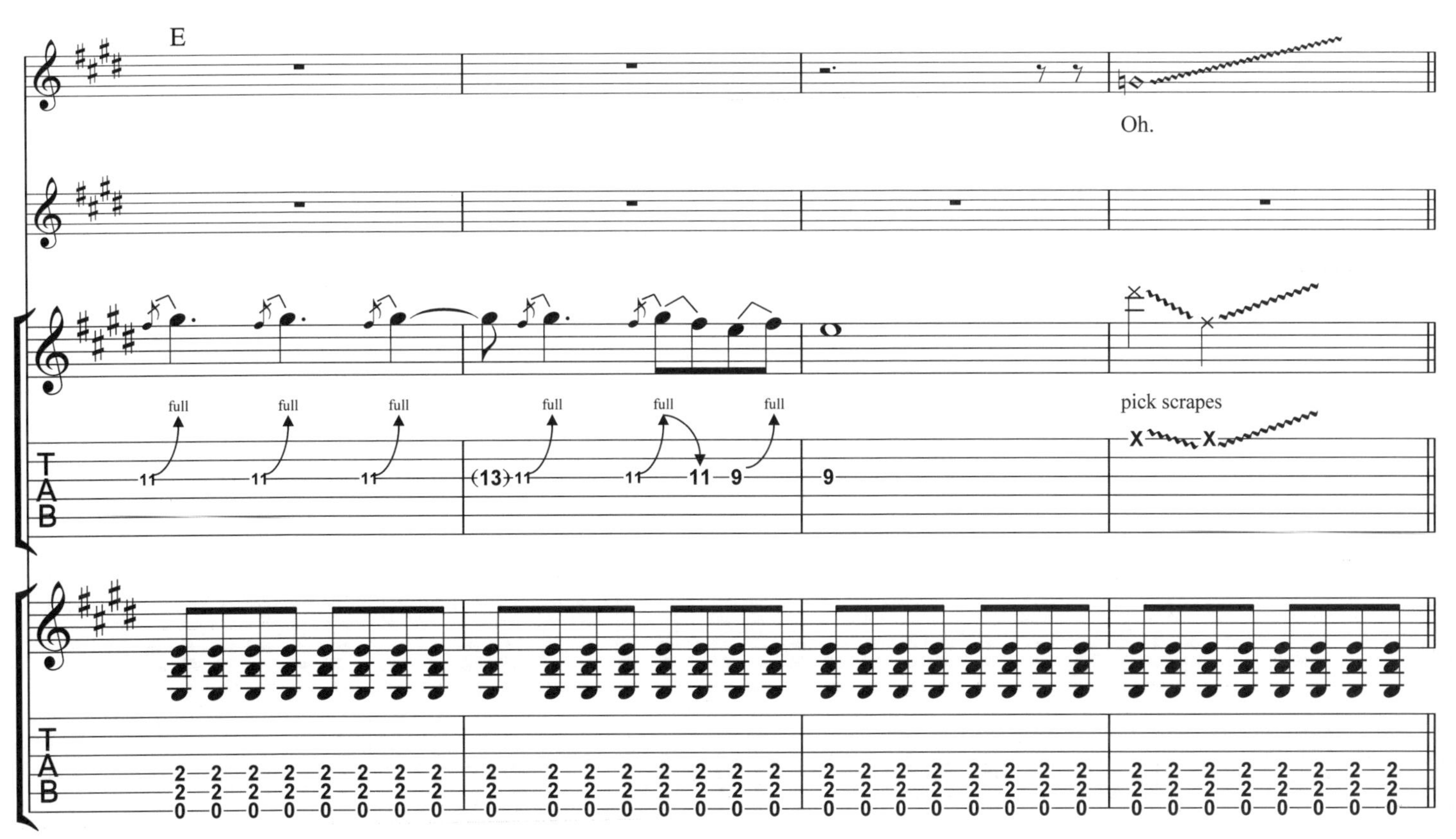

B
A
It does not move me, it's not the kind of thing that I like.
E
2° only
oh
Na na na na naa.
Na na na na naa.
Gtrs. 1 + 3

Verse
A
E
It does not move me, it does not get me go - ing at all.
It does not move me, at all.
Gtr. 3 tacet
w/clean bell-like tone
let ring
A
It does not shift me,
It does not
let ring

E
it's not the kind of thing that I like.
shift me, I like.
let ring
B
It does not move me, it's
Oh.
w/distortion

A
not the kind of thing that I like.

E
Na na na na naa.

Gtrs. 1 + 3 to end

2° only
Oh.

Na na na na naa.

You Can Have It All

Words & Music by Nicholas Hodgson, Richard Wilson,
Andrew White, James Rix & Nicholas Baines

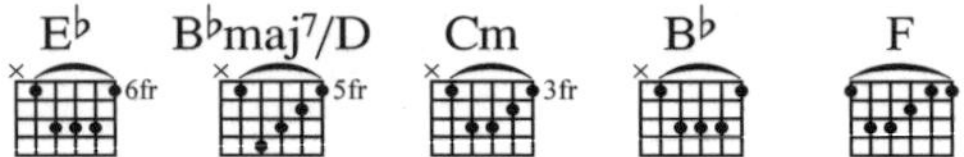

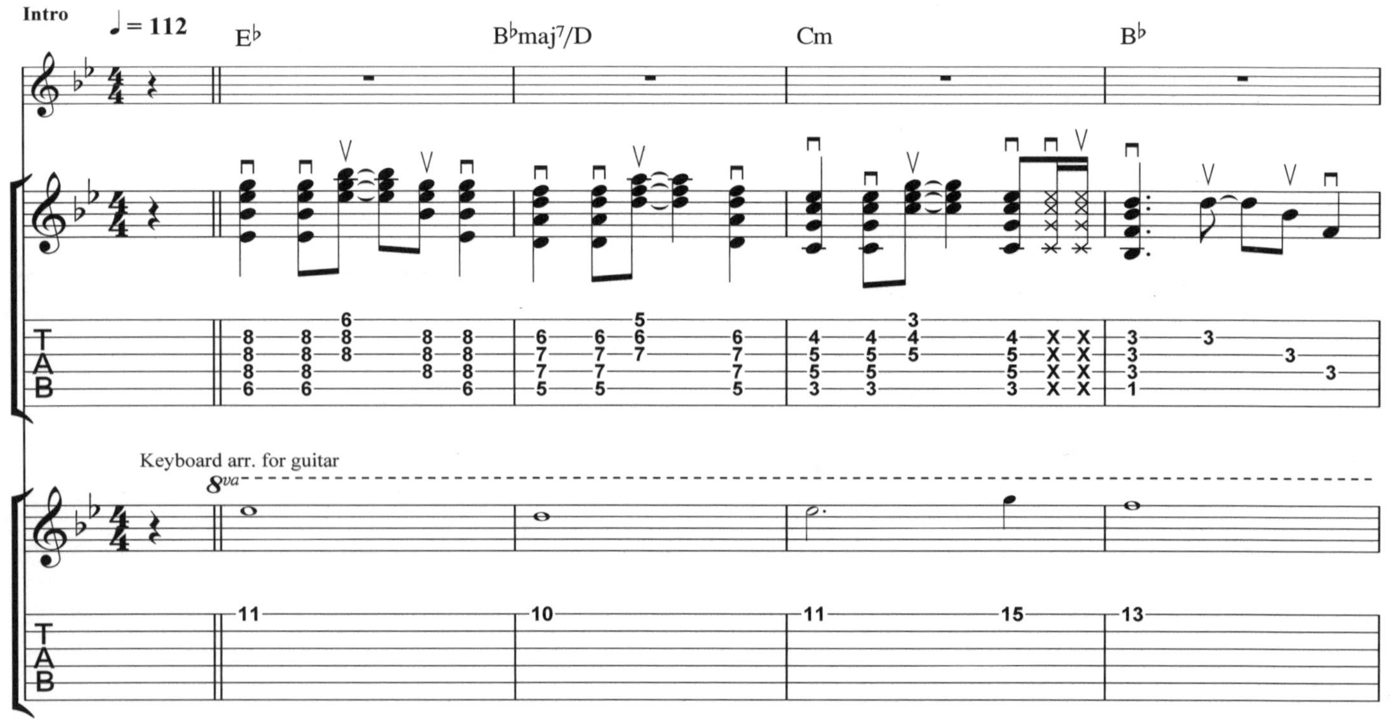

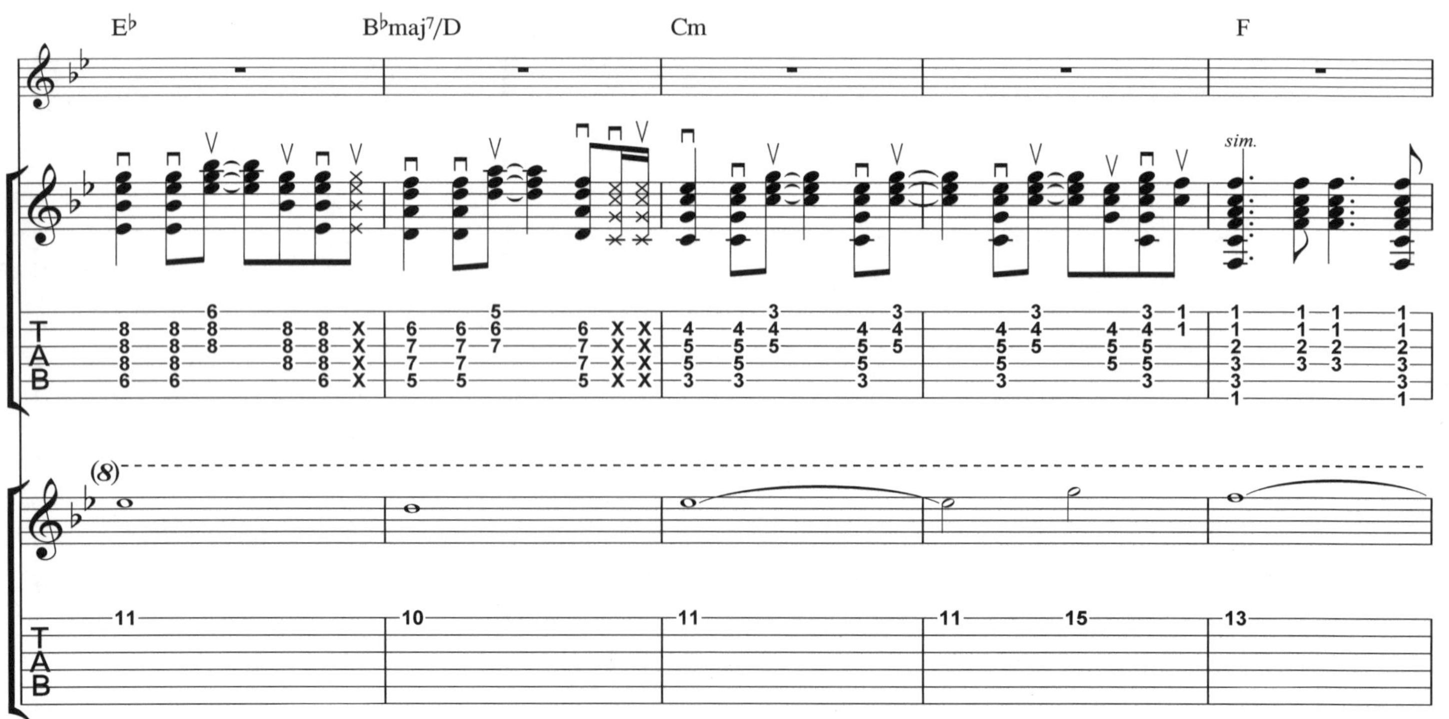

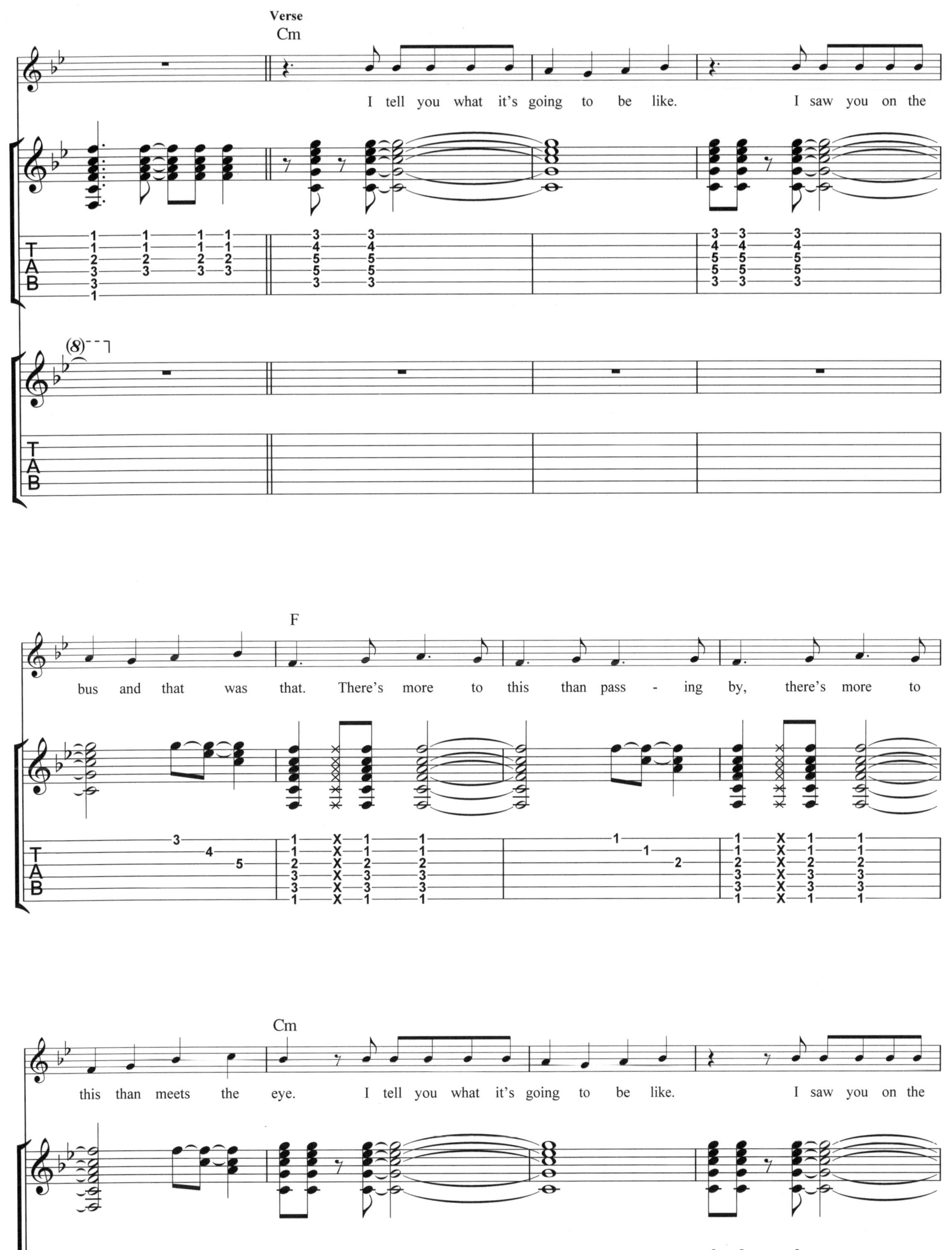
Verse
Cm
I tell you what it's going to be like. I saw you on the
TAB
(8)
TAB
F
bus and that was that. There's more to this than pass - ing by, there's more to
TAB
Cm
this than meets the eye. I tell you what it's going to be like. I saw you on the
TAB

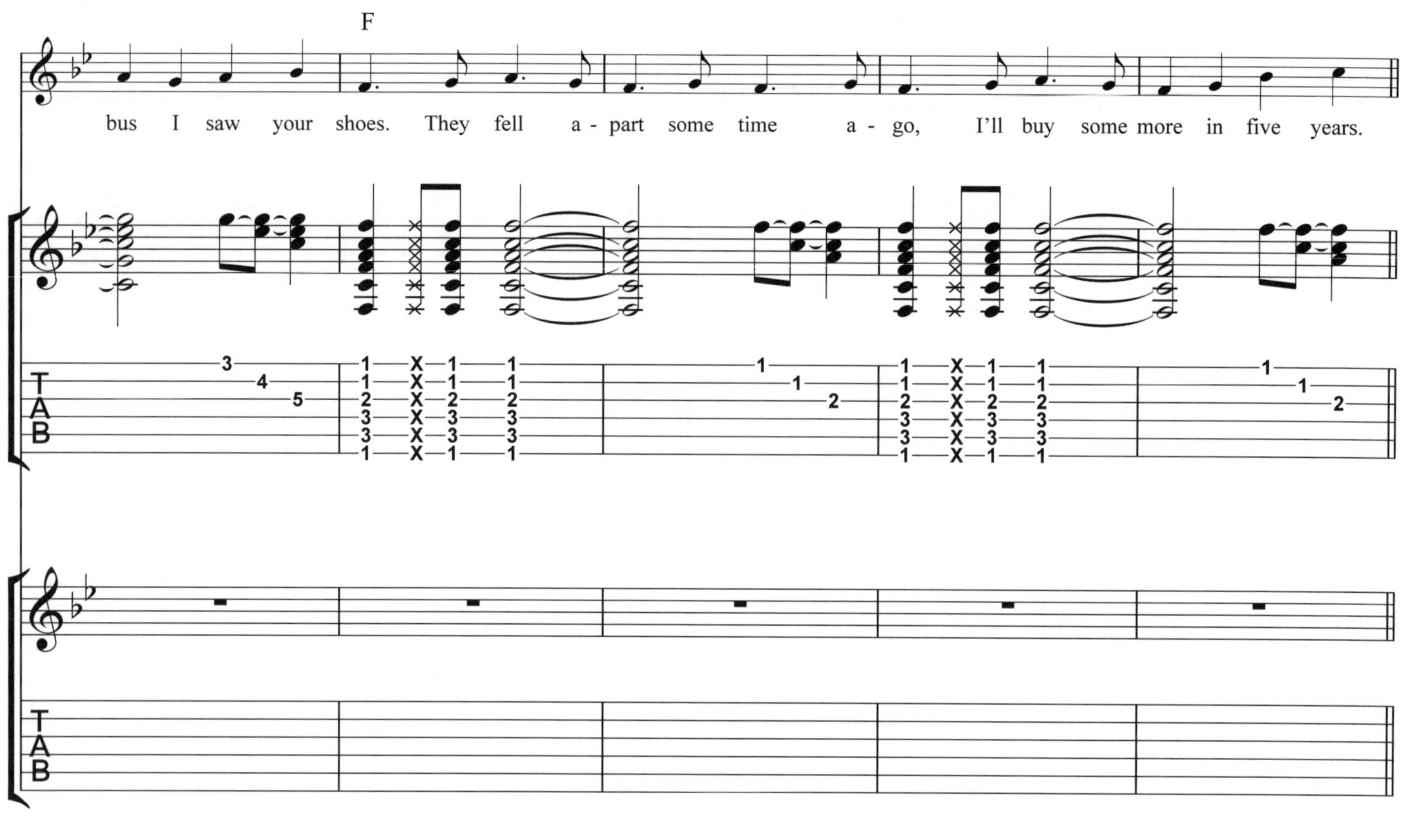

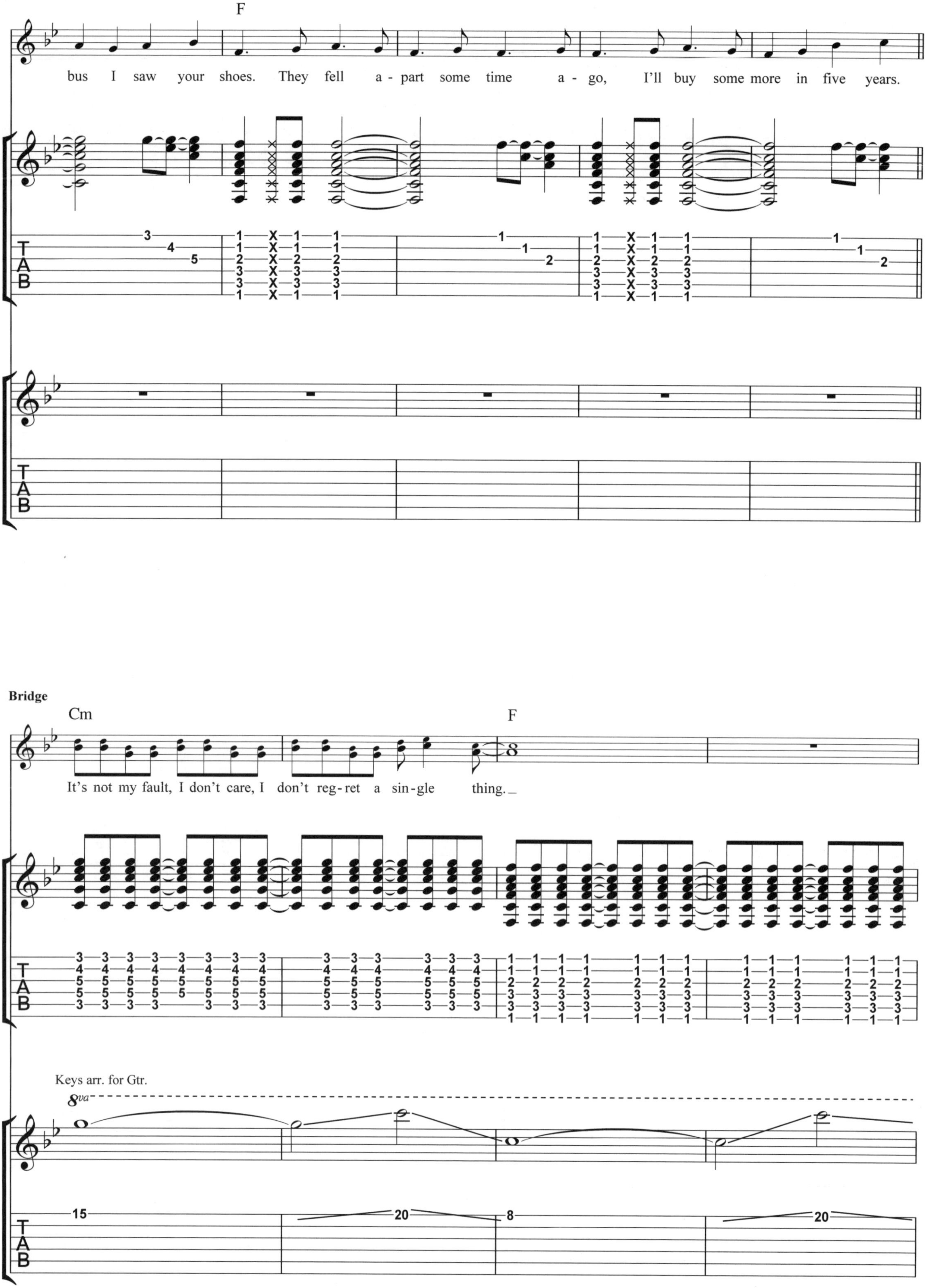

Bridge

Cm F

It's not my fault, I don't care, I don't reg-ret a sin-gle thing._

Keys arr. for Gtr.

8va

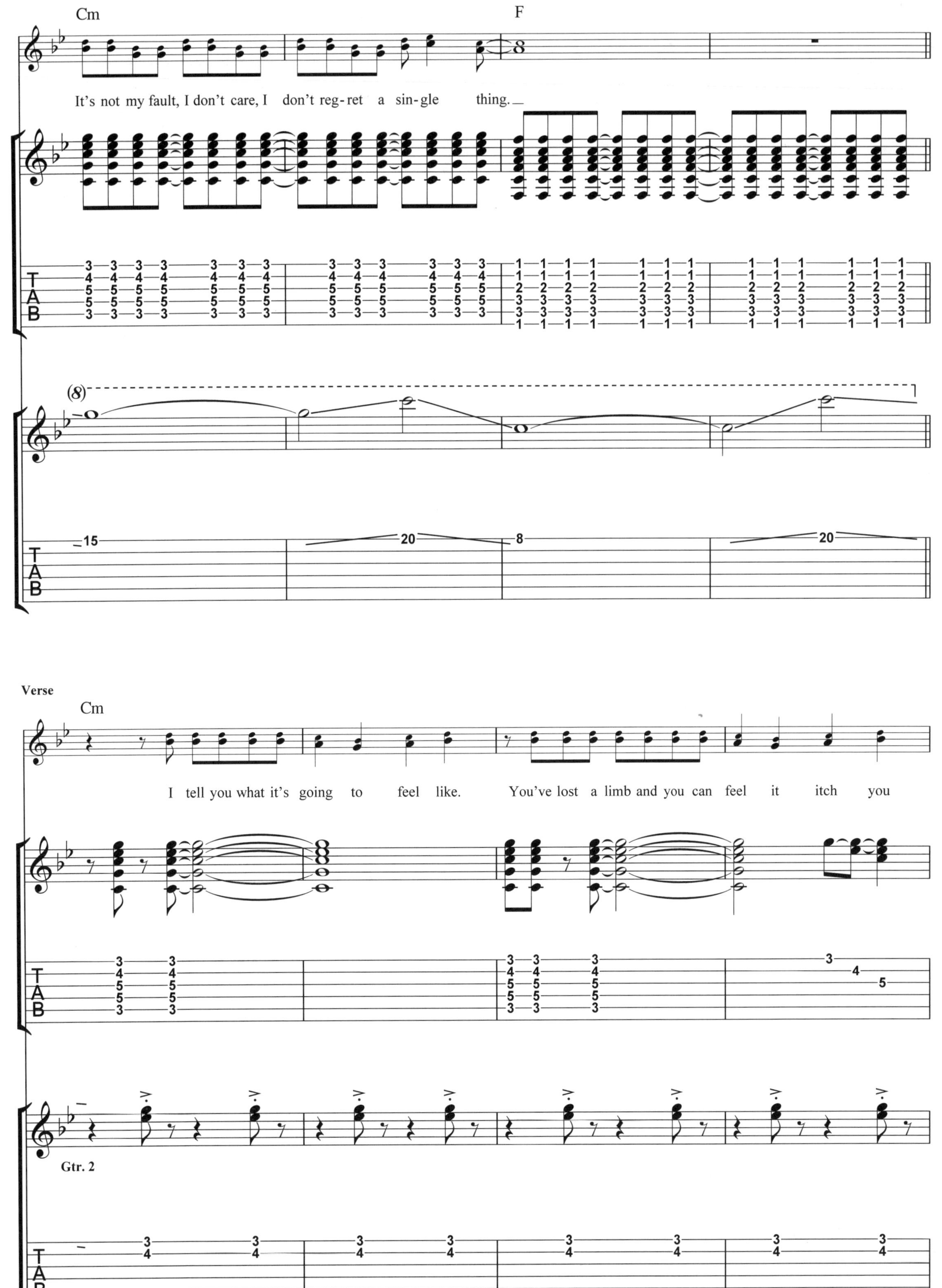

Cm
F
It's not my fault, I don't care, I don't reg-ret a sin-gle thing.
(8)
Verse
Cm
I tell you what it's going to feel like. You've lost a limb and you can feel it itch you
Gtr. 2

F

late at night, not by my side 'cos I'm not there to hold you too tight -

Cm

- ly. I tell you what it's going to be like, though you can ne - ver hold my hand in pub - lic.

F
They can't know or un - der-stand that you and me are now to - geth - er.
Bridge
Cm
F
It's not my fault, I don't care, I don't reg-ret a sin-gle thing.
Keys arr. for Gtr.
8va

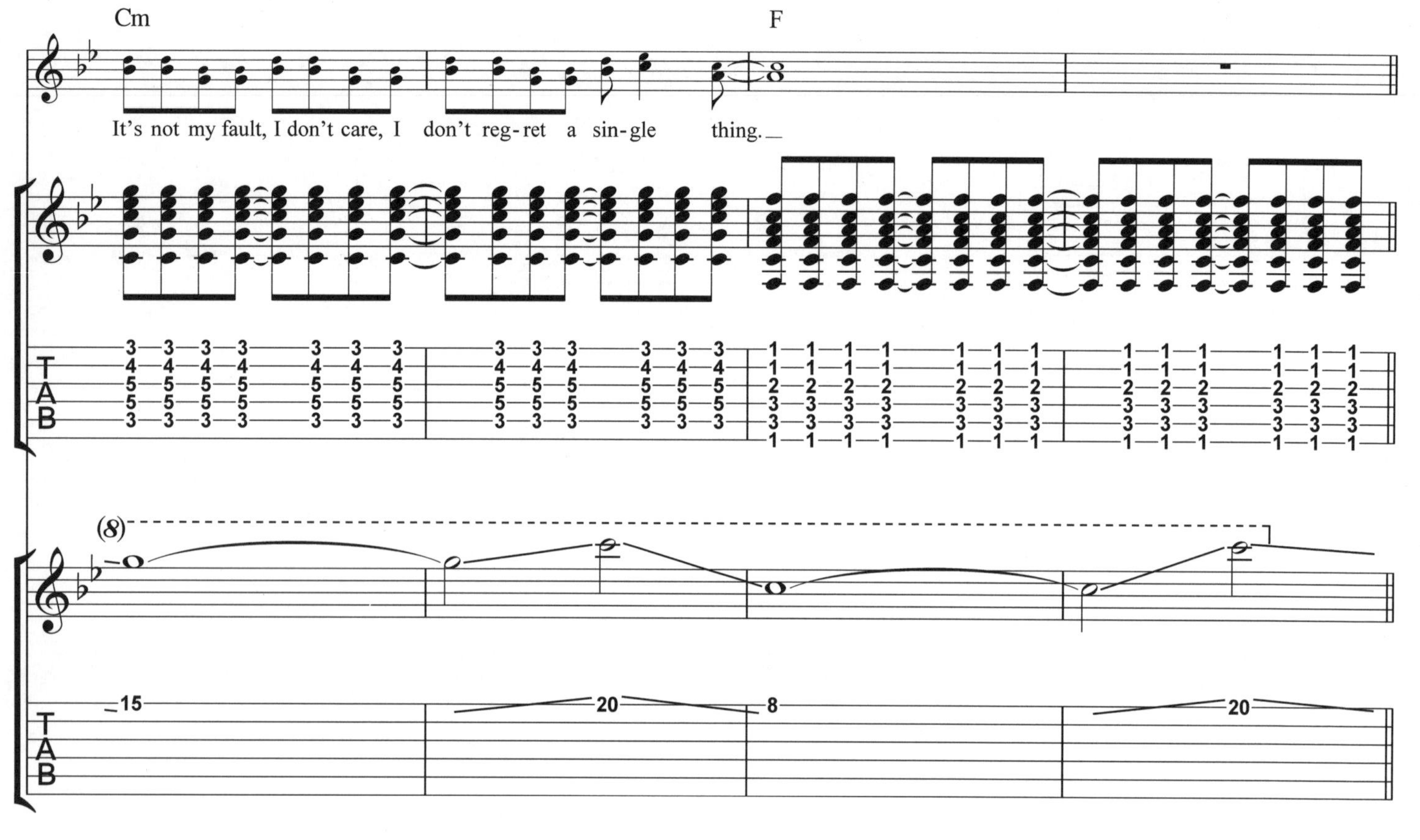
Cm
F
It's not my fault, I don't care, I don't reg-ret a sin-gle thing.

Chorus

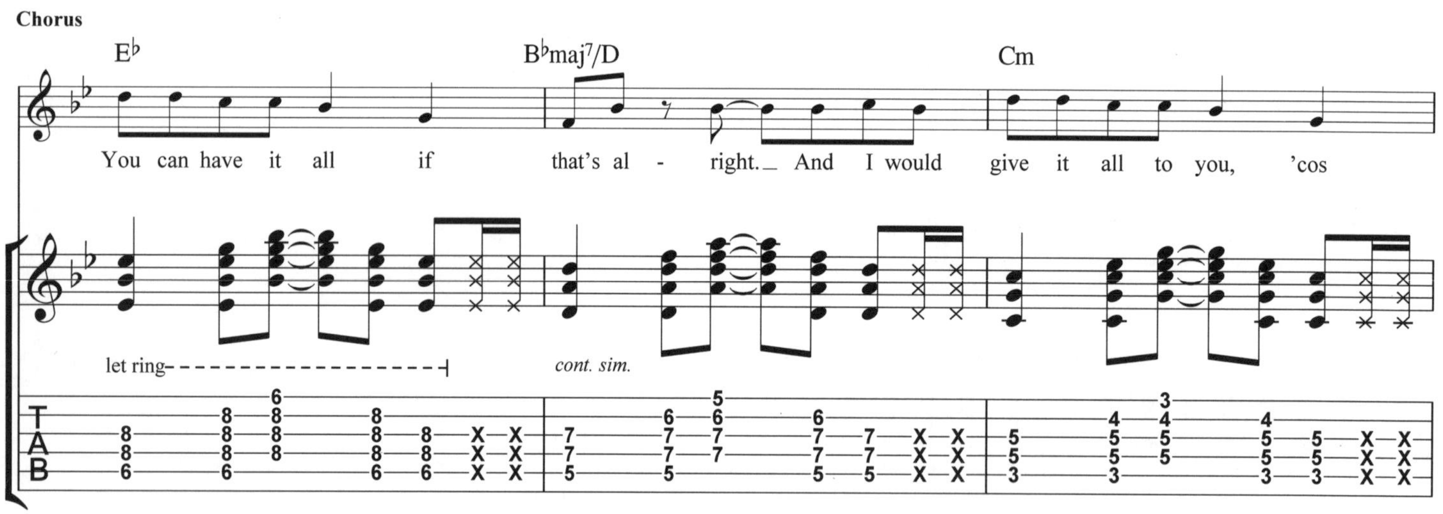
E♭
B♭maj7/D
Cm
You can have it all if that's al - right. And I would give it all to you, 'cos
let ring
cont. sim.

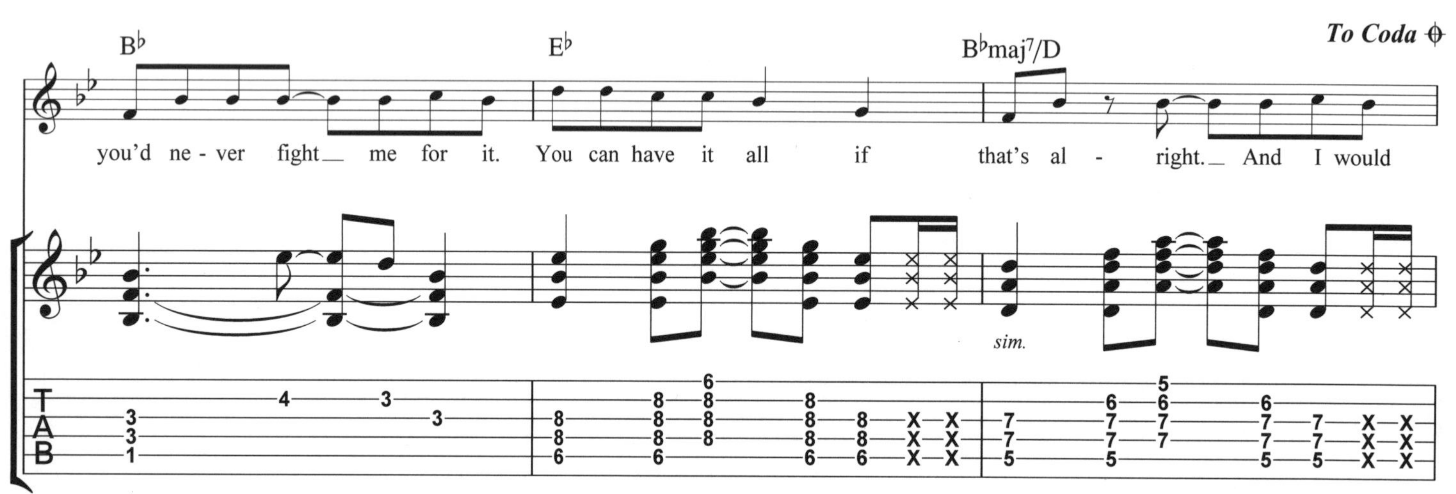
B♭
E♭
B♭maj7/D
To Coda
you'd ne - ver fight me for it. You can have it all if that's al - right. And I would
sim.

Cm
F
give it all to you
if it's all
right?
Oh oh oh
Gtr. solo
Cm
Gtr. 2
F

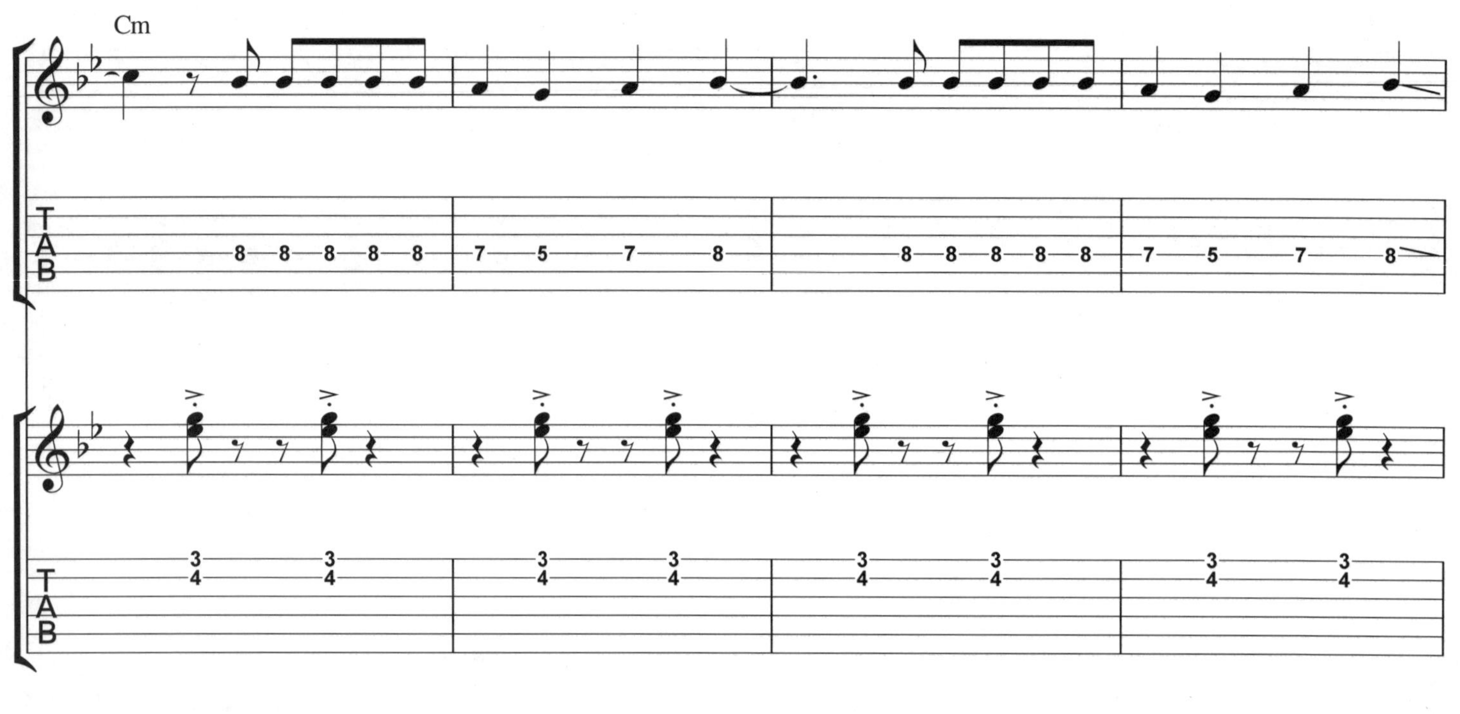
Cm

F
D.S. al Coda

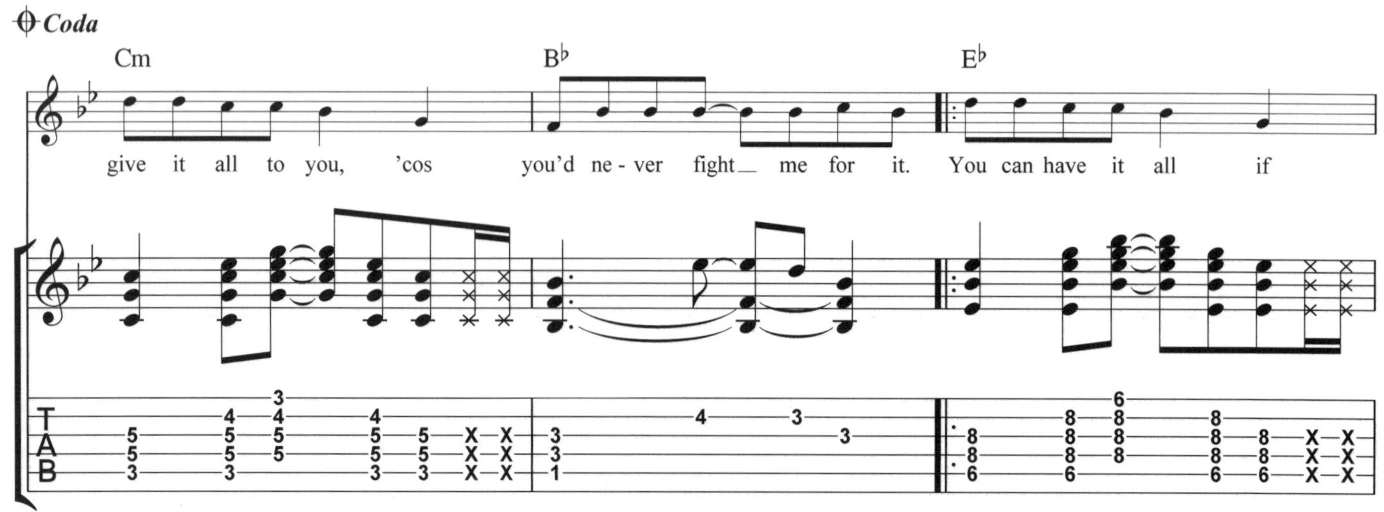
Coda
Cm
B♭
E♭
give it all to you, 'cos you'd ne - ver fight_ me for it. You can have it all if

1.

B♭maj7/D | Cm | B♭

that's al - right. And I would give it all to you, 'cos you'd ne - ver fight me for it.

cont. sim.

2.

Cm | F

give it all to you if it's all right? Oh oh oh.

Outro

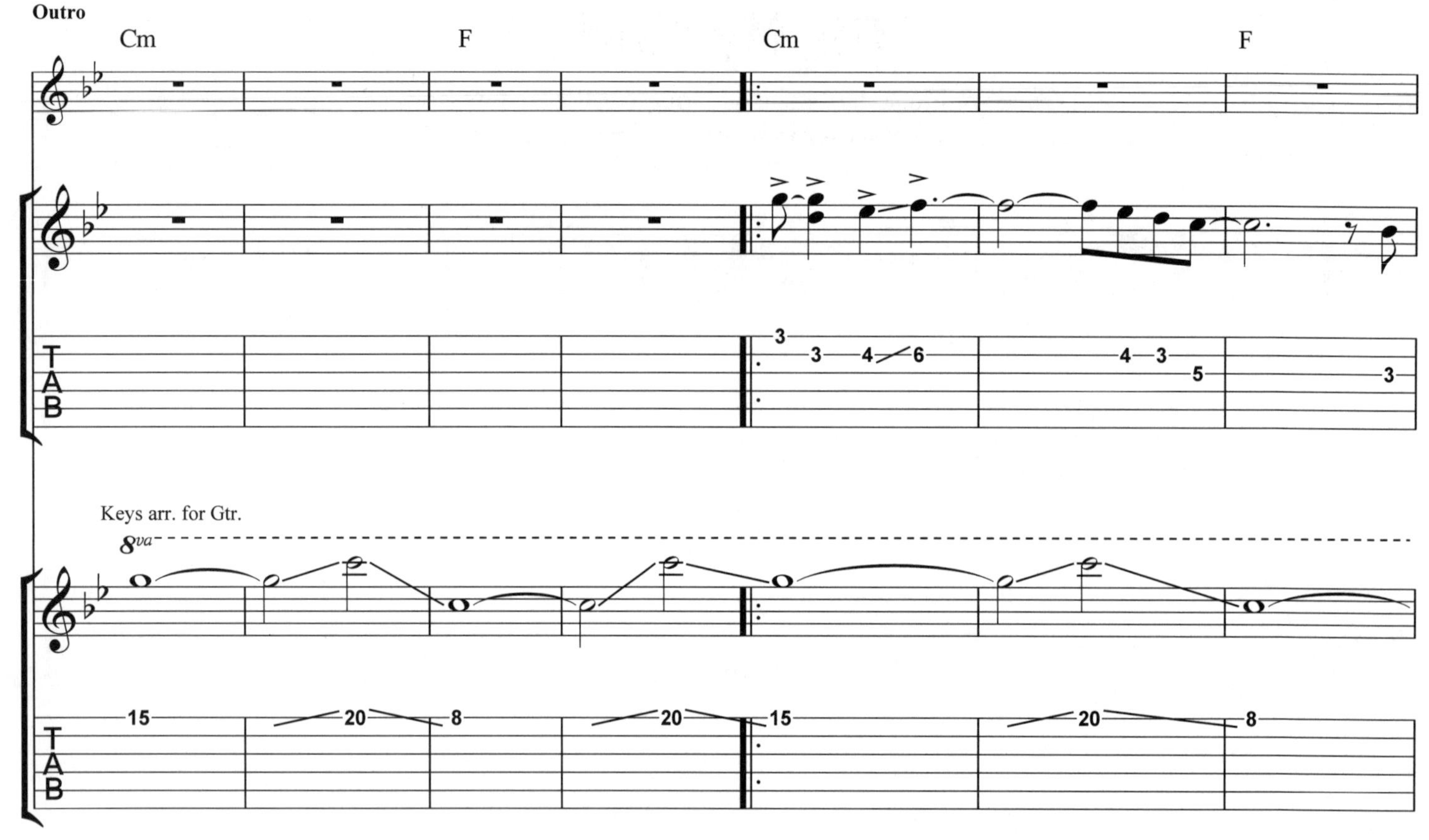

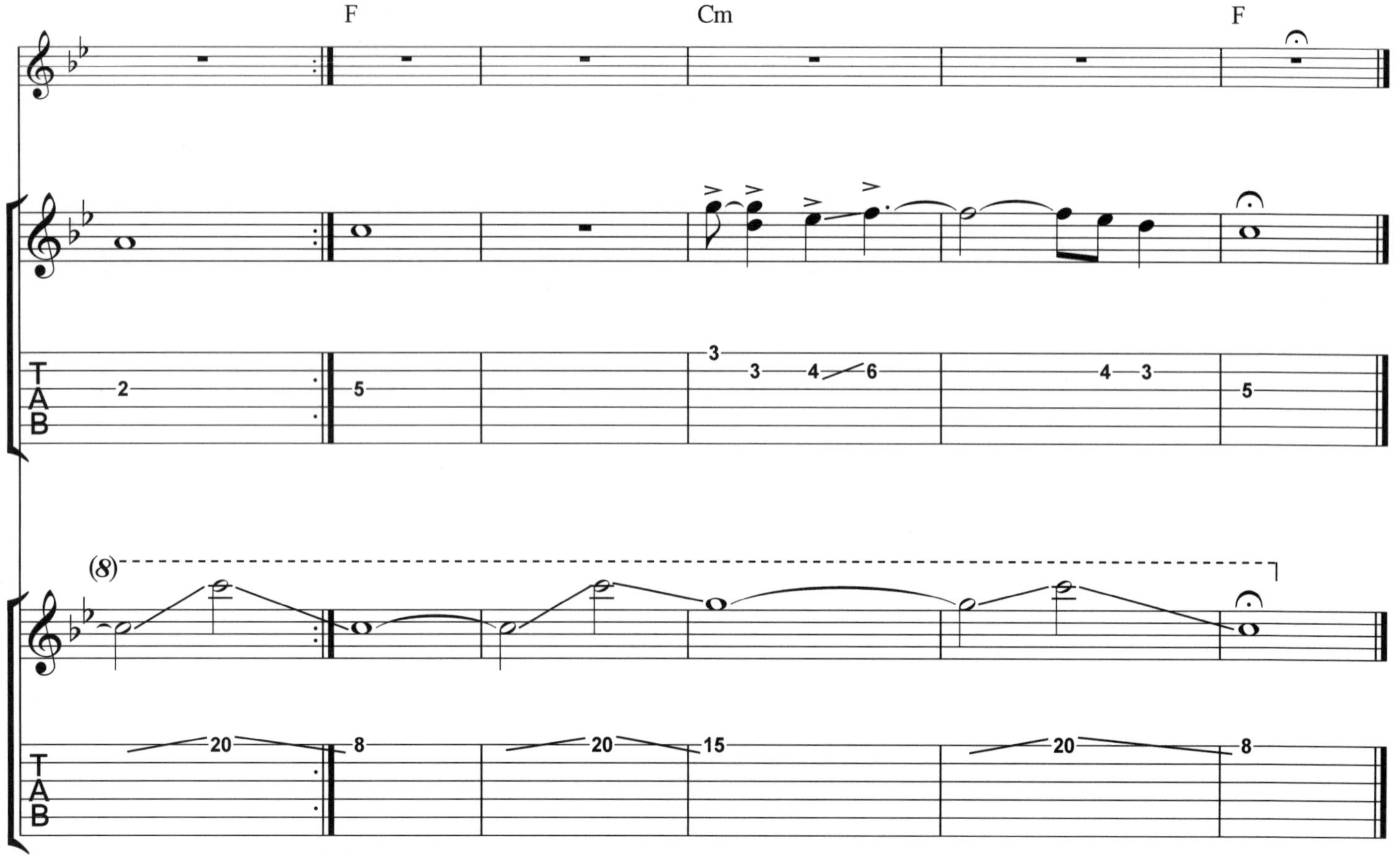

F
Cm
F
(8)

Oh My God

Words & Music by Nicholas Hodgson, Richard Wilson, Andrew White, James Rix & Nicholas Baines

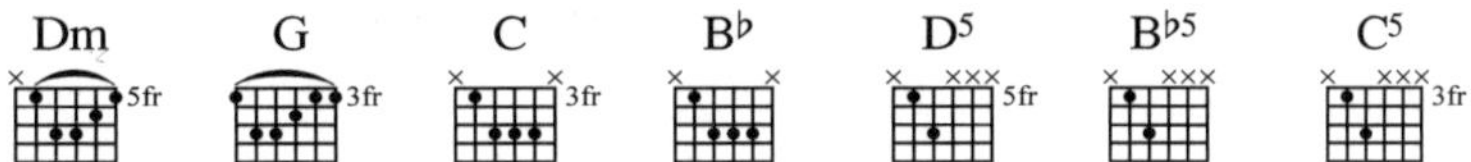

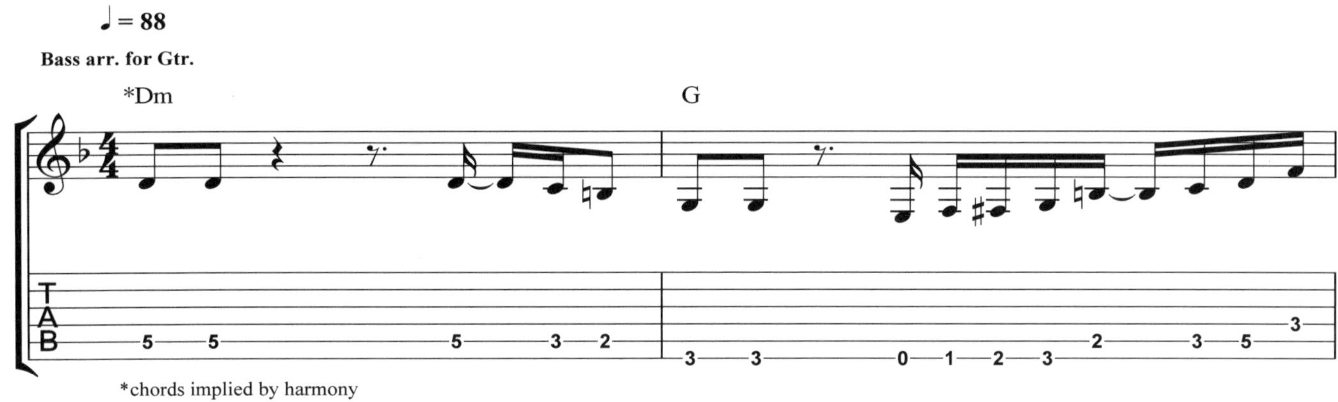

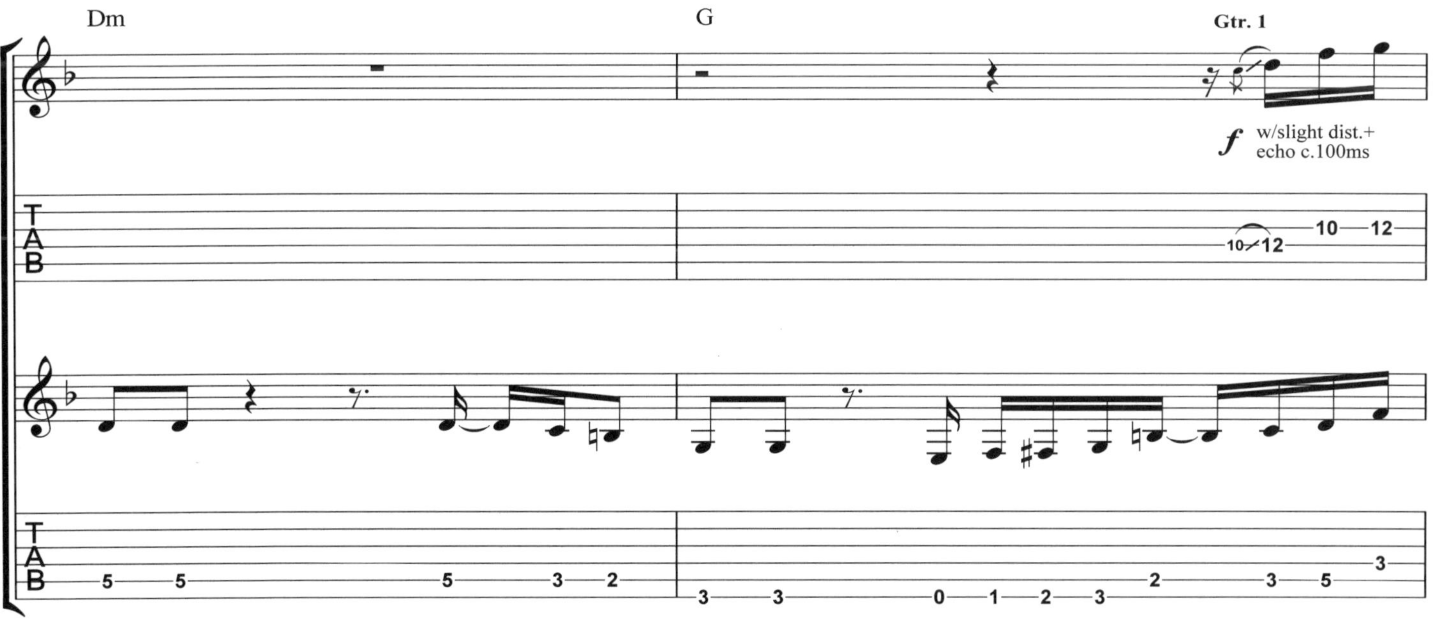

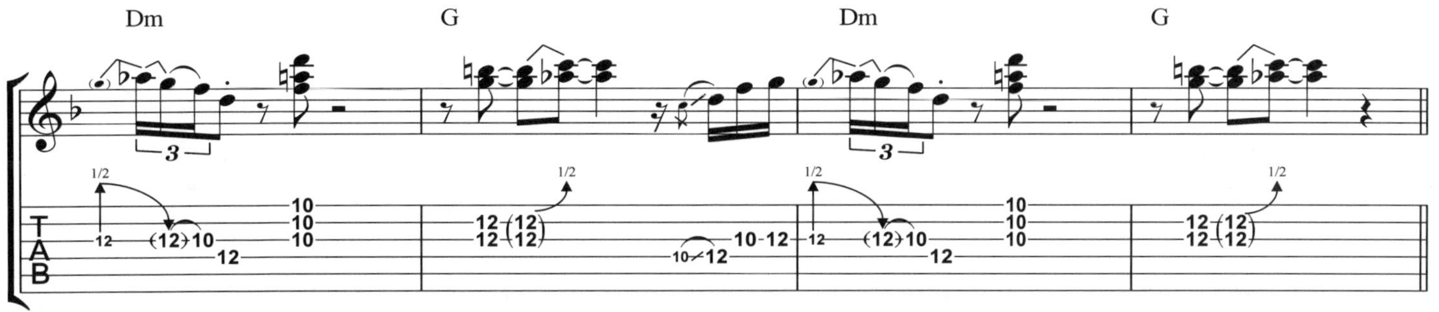

Verse
Dm
G
1. Time on your side, it will nev - er end. The most beau - ti-ful thing you can ev - er spend. But you
2. Too much time spent drag-ging the past up, I did-n't see you not look-ing when I messed up.
3. Great ru-ins meant for great - er glo-ries, the on-ly thing grow-ing is our his - to - ry.
cancel echo
work in a shirt with your name tag on it, drift - ing a-part like a plate tec - ton - ic.
Set - tl-ing down in your ear - ly twen - ties, sucked more blood than a back - street dent - ist.
Knock me down, I'll get right back up a-gain. Come back strong-er like a pow-ered up pac-man.
Pre-Chorus
G
Dm
C
B♭
It don't mat-ter to me. 'Cos all I want-ed to be, was a
mil - li - on miles from here. Some - where more fa - mi -

1.
2, 3.
B♭
- li - ar.
Chorus
D5
B♭5
C5
Oh my God I can't be - lieve it, I've nev - er been this far a - way from home. And
Gtr. 2
Gtr. 2 w/dist.
Gtr. 1 tacet
oh my God I can't be - lieve it, I've nev - er been this far a - way from home. And
oh my God I can't be - lieve it, I've nev - er been this far a - way from home. And

D5
1.
B♭5
C5
oh my God I can't be - lieve it, I've nev - er been this far a - way from home.
2.
Interlude
G
Dm
C
B♭
nev - er been this far a - way from home.
Gtr. 1
Gtr. 1 w/clean tone + echo
Gtr. 2 tacet
8va

Chorus
D5
Bb5
C5
Oh my God I can't be - lieve it, I've nev - er been this far a - way from home. And
Gtr. 2
f Gtr. 2 w/dist.
Gtr. 1 tacet

D5
Bb5
C5
oh my God I can't be - lieve it, I've nev - er been this far a - way from home. And

D5
Bb5
C5
oh my God I can't be - lieve it, I've nev - er been this far a - way from home. And

D5
Bb5
C5
D5
oh my God I can't be - lieve it, I've nev - er been this far a - way from home.

Born To Be A Dancer

Words & Music by Nicholas Hodgson, Richard Wilson, Andrew White, James Rix & Nicholas Baines

Chorus
G5
F5
B♭5
A♭5
Once you asked me what I'm think - ing, I lay back and think of Eng - land.
Do you know my re - al ans - wer, I was born to be a dan - cer.
Oh oh oh oh oh o oh oh Oh oh oh oh oh o oh oh
Verse
(Dm)
(B♭)
I came down at your (on the Na - tio - nal Ex - press) re - quest, to touch your breasts. And
Gtr. 2 cont. sim. (Piano arr.)

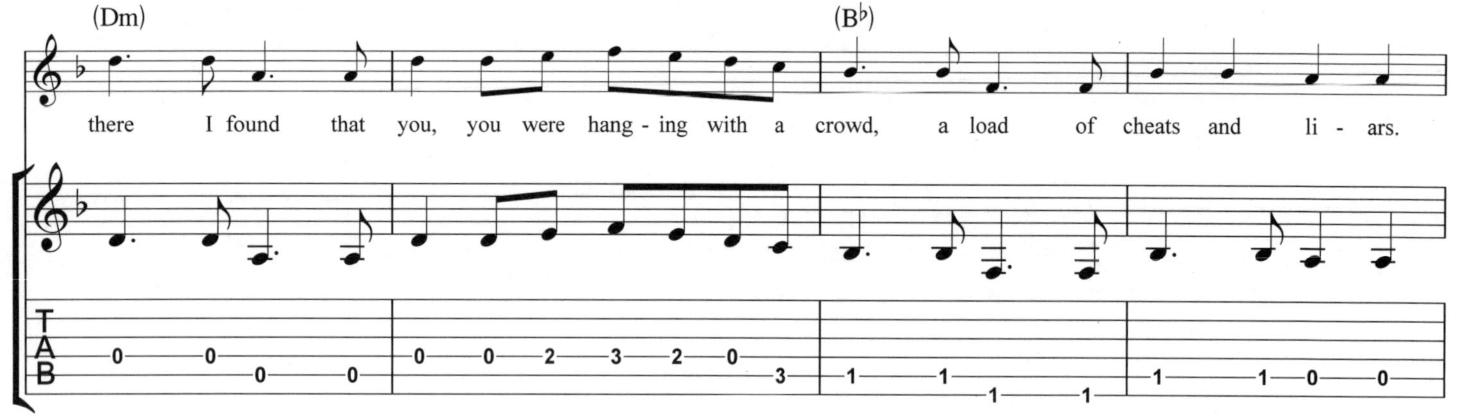
(Dm)
(B♭)
there I found that you, you were hang - ing with a crowd, a load of cheats and li - ars.

Chorus

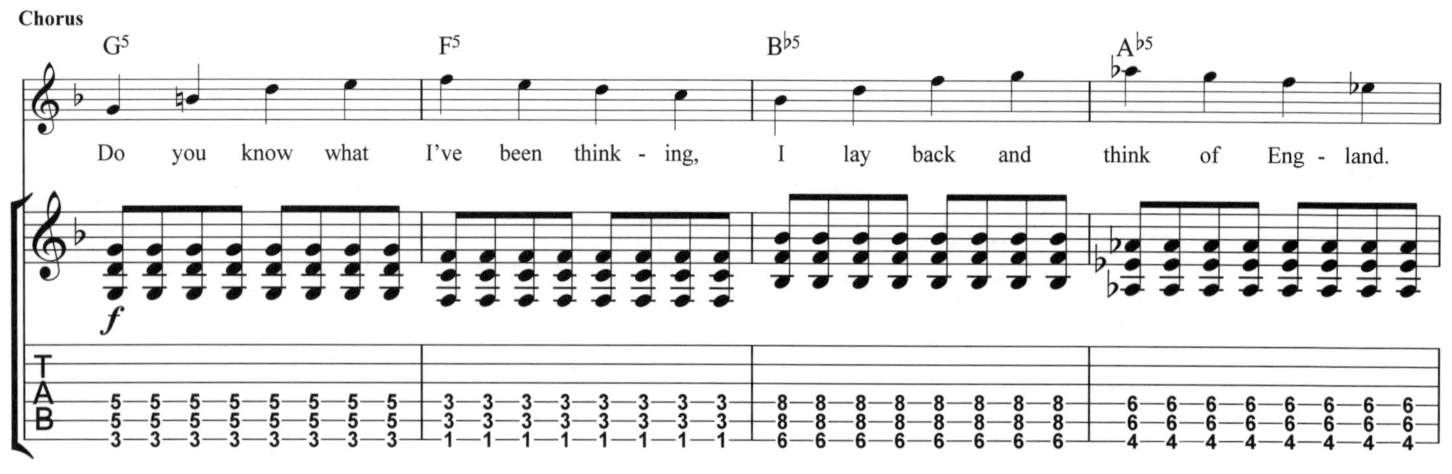
G5 F5 B♭5 A♭5
Do you know what I've been think - ing, I lay back and think of Eng - land.

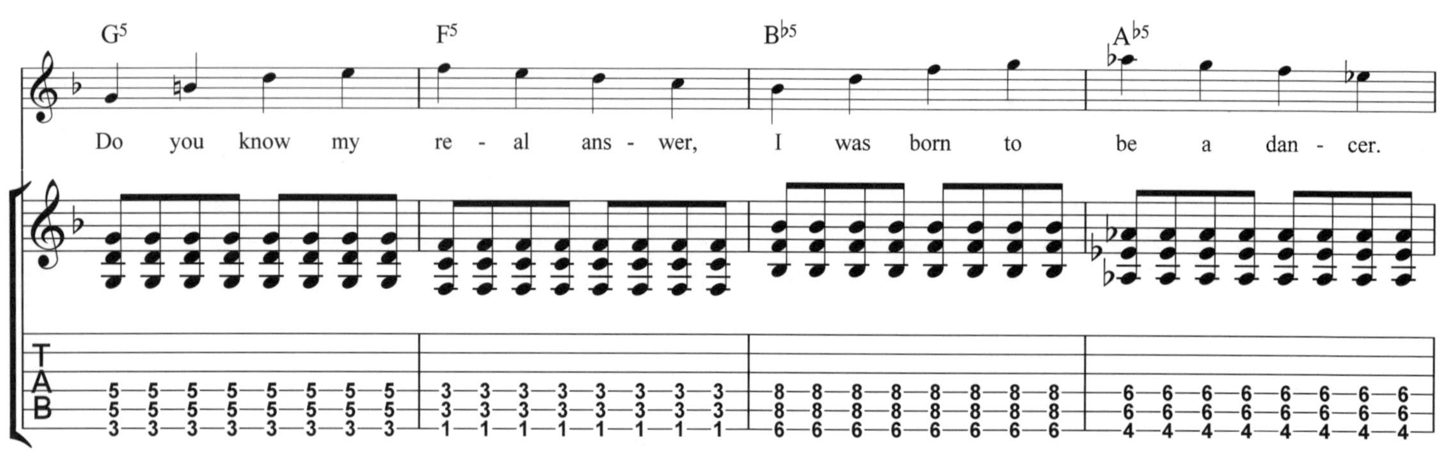
G5 F5 B♭5 A♭5
Do you know my re - al ans - wer, I was born to be a dan - cer.

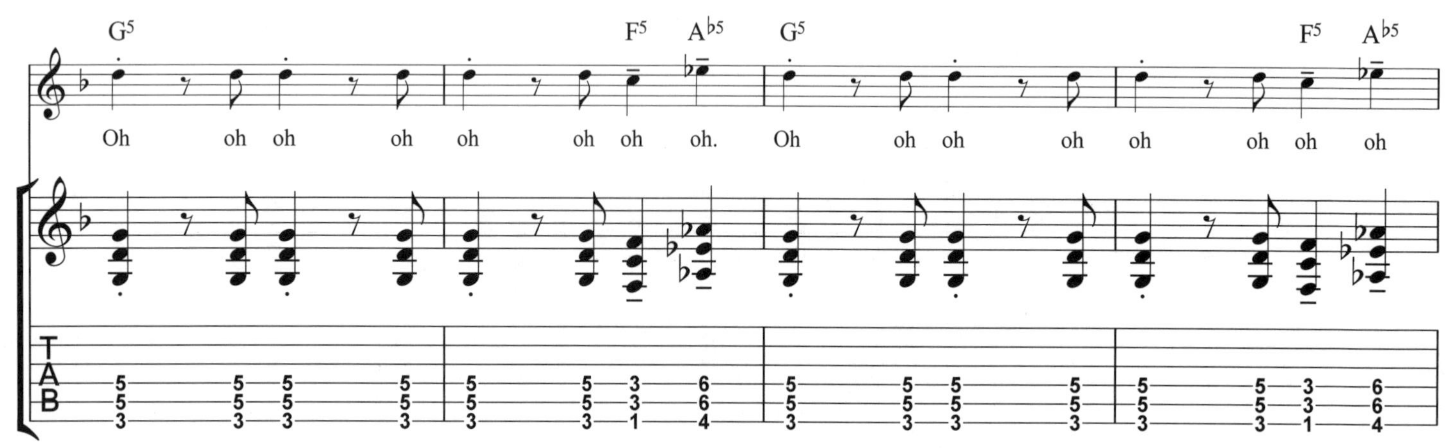
G5 F5 A♭5 G5 F5 A♭5
Oh oh oh oh oh oh oh oh. Oh oh oh oh oh oh oh oh

B♭5
A♭5
E♭5
Oh oh oh oh oh oh oh oh Oh oh oh oh oh oh oh oh
*(Dm)
(B♭)
(Dm) (Dm/E) (Dm/F) (Dm/G)
Guitar solo
*Chords implied by harmony
(A)
Ah.
(2º only)
A
Chorus
G
F
Once you asked me what I'm think - ing,

B♭
A♭
G
F
I lay back and think of Eng - land. Do you know my re - al ans - wer,
B♭
A♭
G
F
I was born to be a dan - cer. Do you know what I've been think - ing,
B♭
A♭
G
F
I lay back and think of Eng - land. Do you know my re - al ans - wer,
B♭
A♭
G5
I was born to be a dan - cer. Oh oh oh oh oh.
T
A
B

Saturday Night

Words & Music by Nicholas Hodgson, Richard Wilson, Andrew White, James Rix & Nicholas Baines

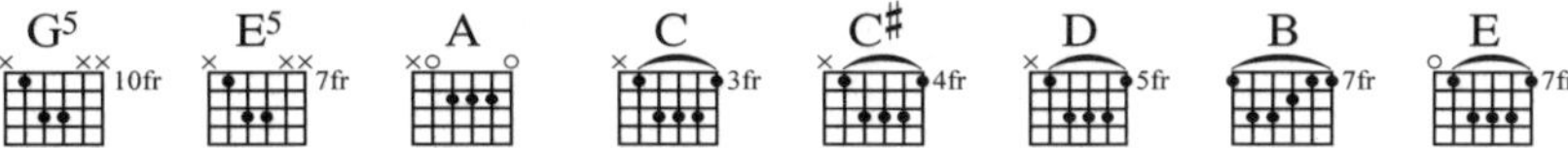

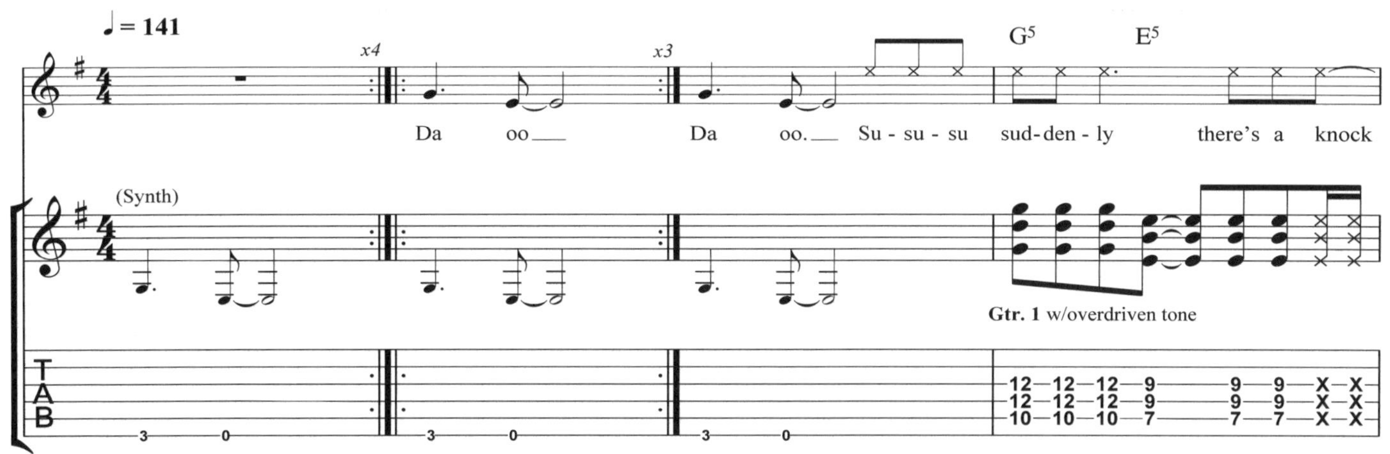

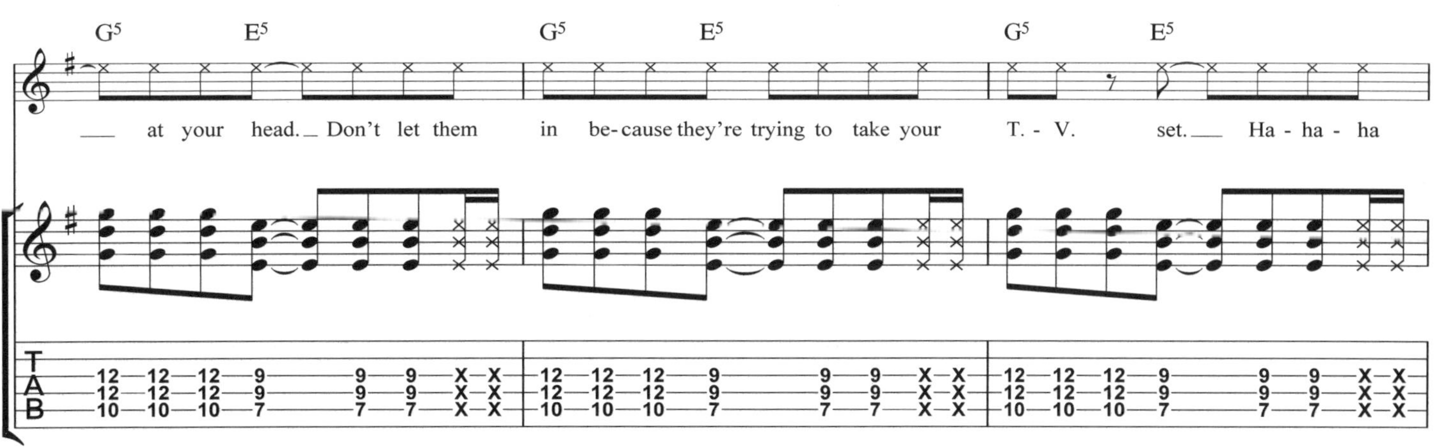

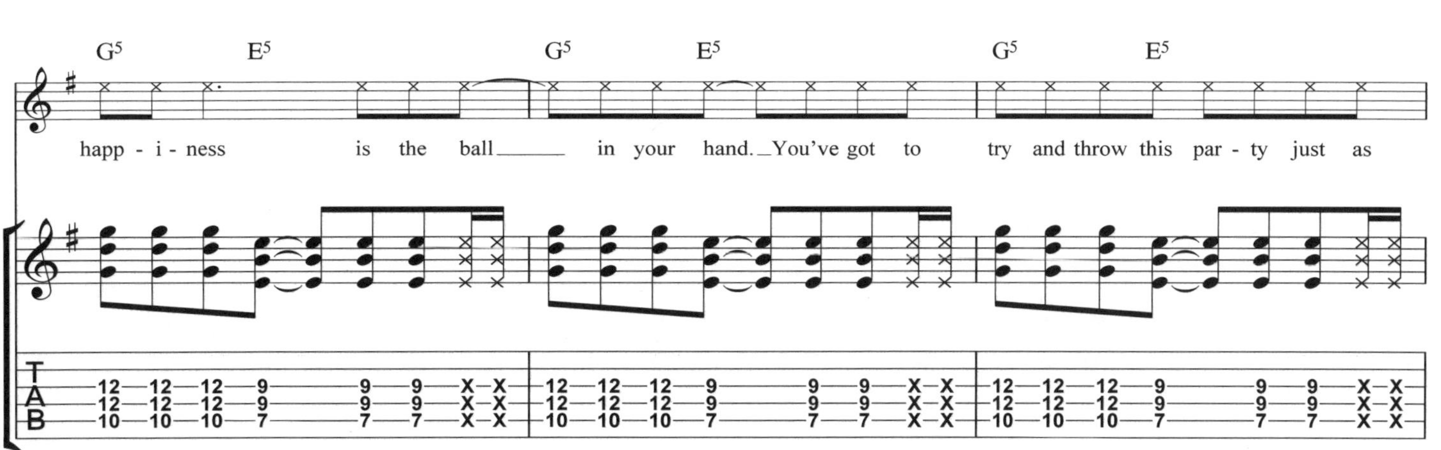

G5 E5 A
far as you can.
G5 E5 G5 E5
C - c - c - cre - o - sote is pour - ing out of my brain, I swear
G5 E5 G5 E5 G5 E5
I heard the floor-boards they were creak - ing your name. G - g - g - get a room, get a head,
G5 E5 G5 E5 G5 E5
get a hat. We're go - ing to Hell an - y - way let's tra - vel first class.

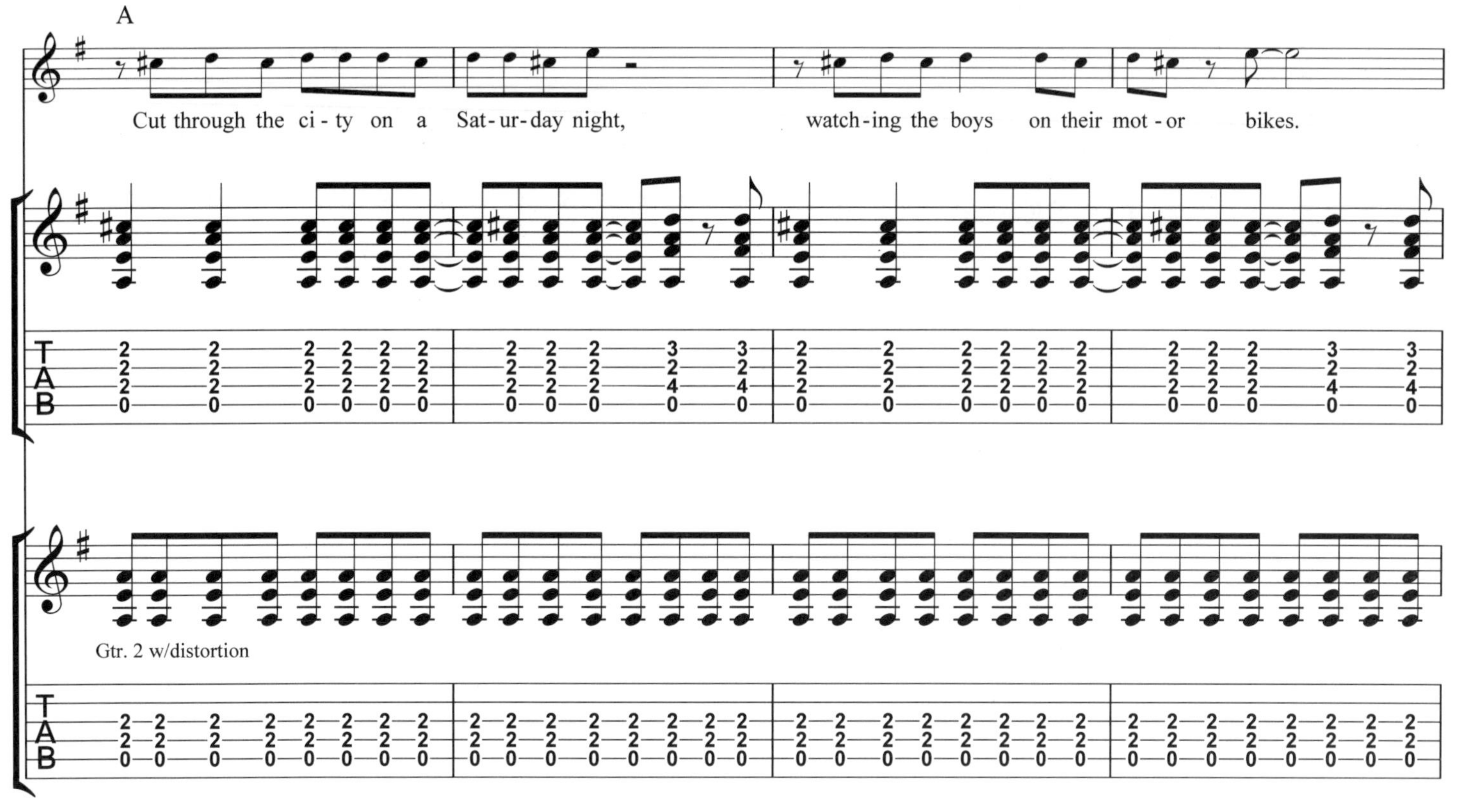
A
Cut through the ci - ty on a Sat - ur - day night, watch - ing the boys on their mot - or bikes.
Gtr. 2 w/distortion

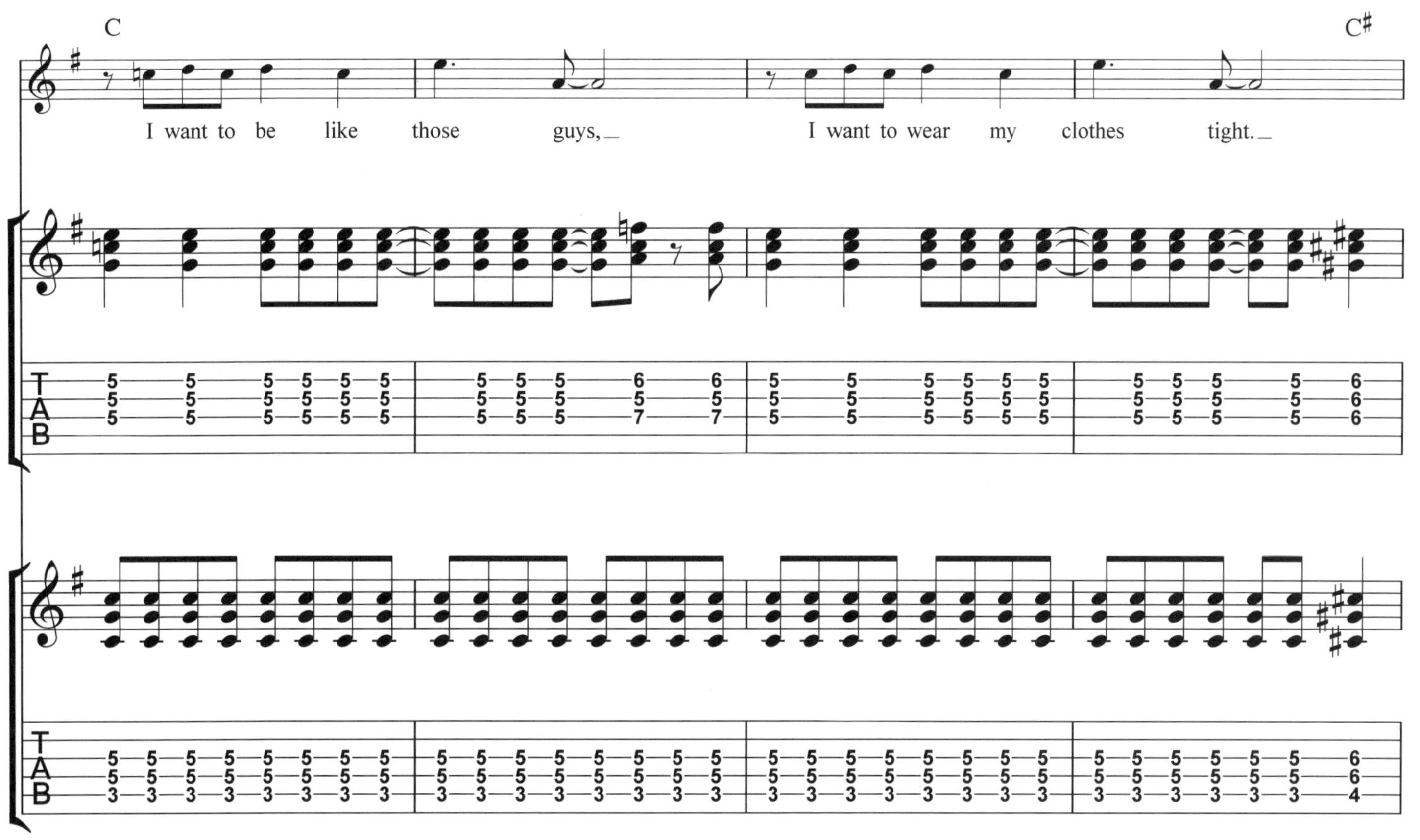
C
C♯
I want to be like those guys, I want to wear my clothes tight.

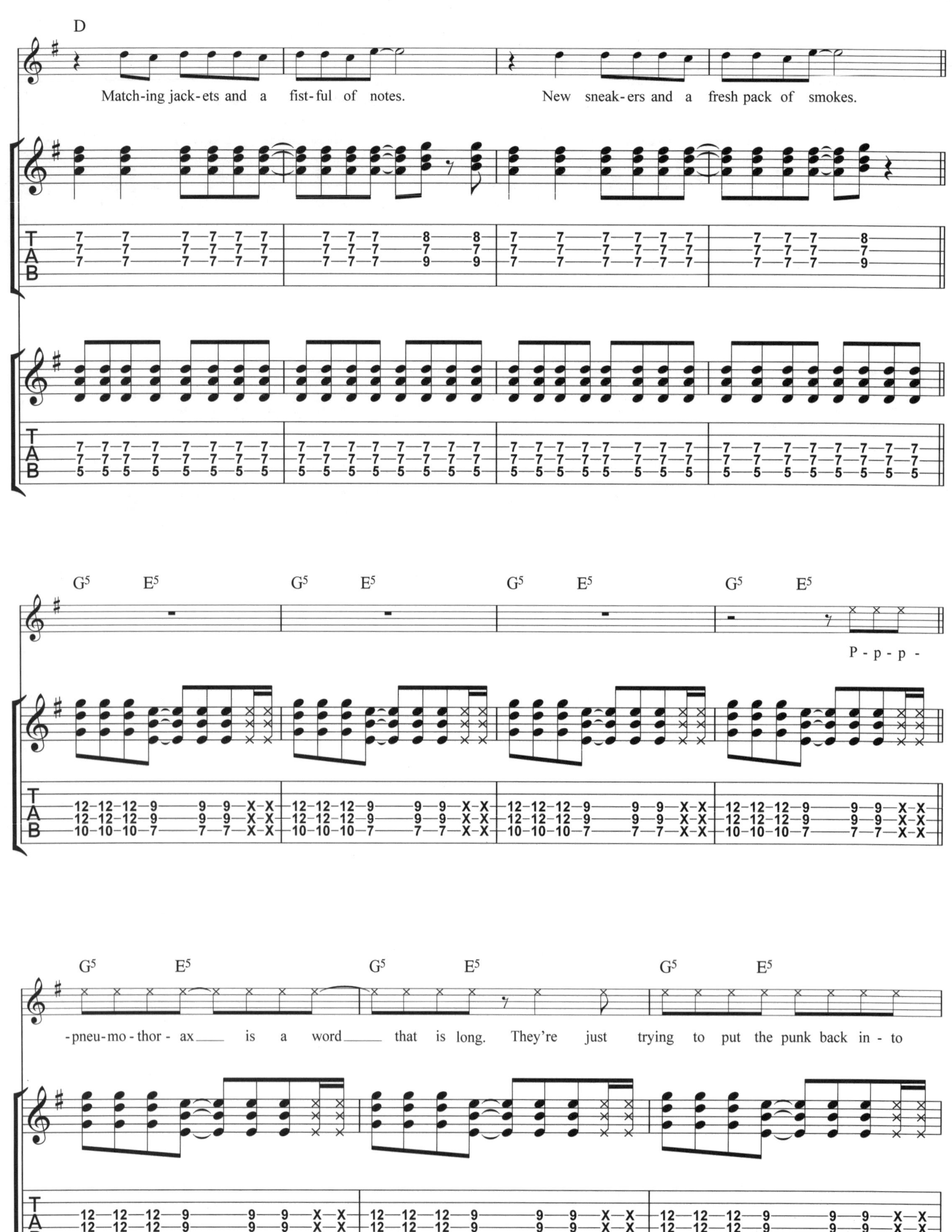
D
Match-ing jack-ets and a fist-ful of notes. New sneak-ers and a fresh pack of smokes.
G5 E5
P - p - p -
-pneu-mo-thor-ax is a word that is long. They're just trying to put the punk back in-to

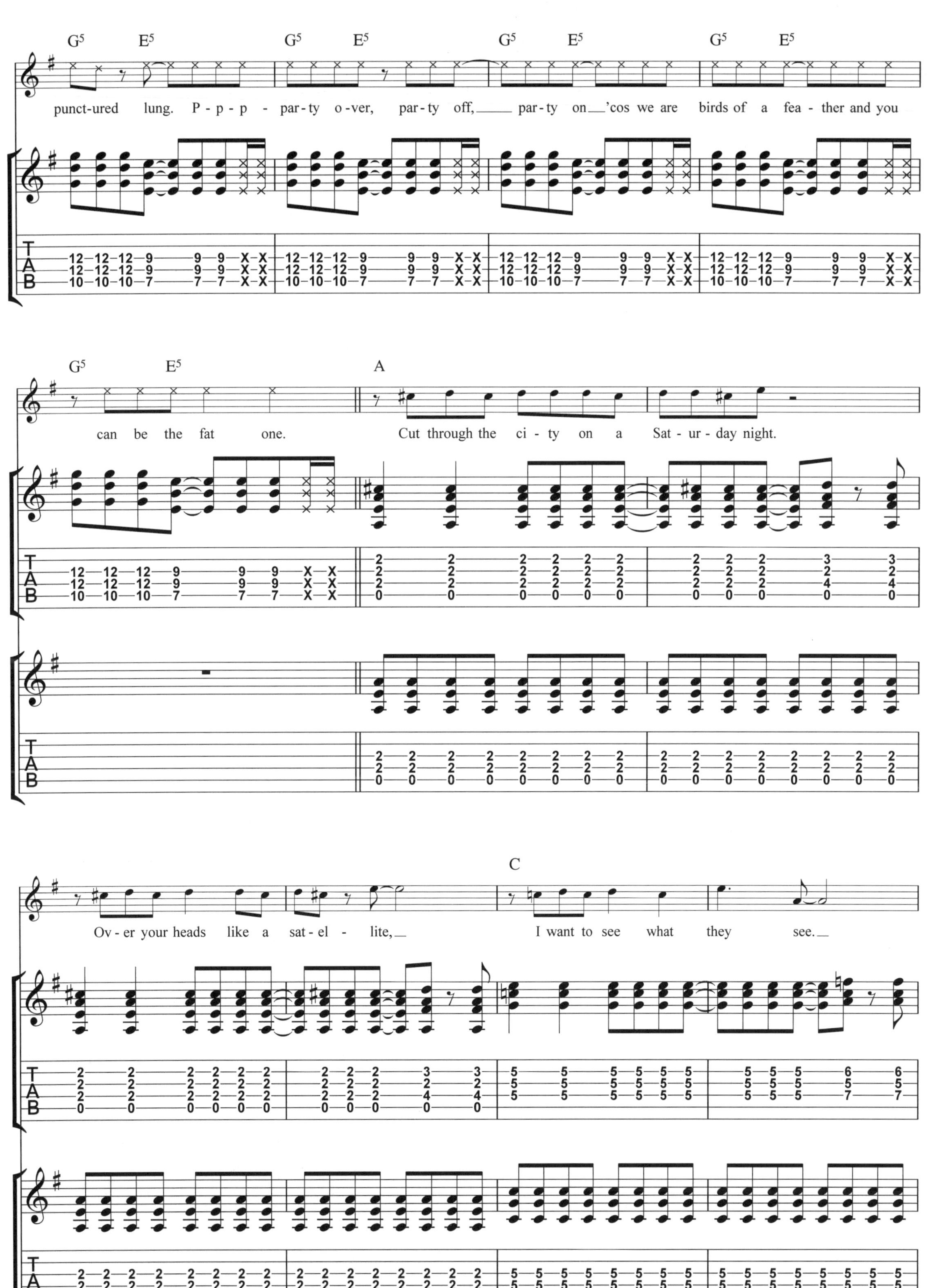

G5 E5 G5 E5 G5 E5 G5 E5
punct-ured lung. P - p - p - par-ty o-ver, par-ty off, par-ty on 'cos we are birds of a fea - ther and you
G5 E5 A
can be the fat one. Cut through the ci - ty on a Sat - ur - day night.
C
Ov - er your heads like a sat - el - lite, I want to see what they see.

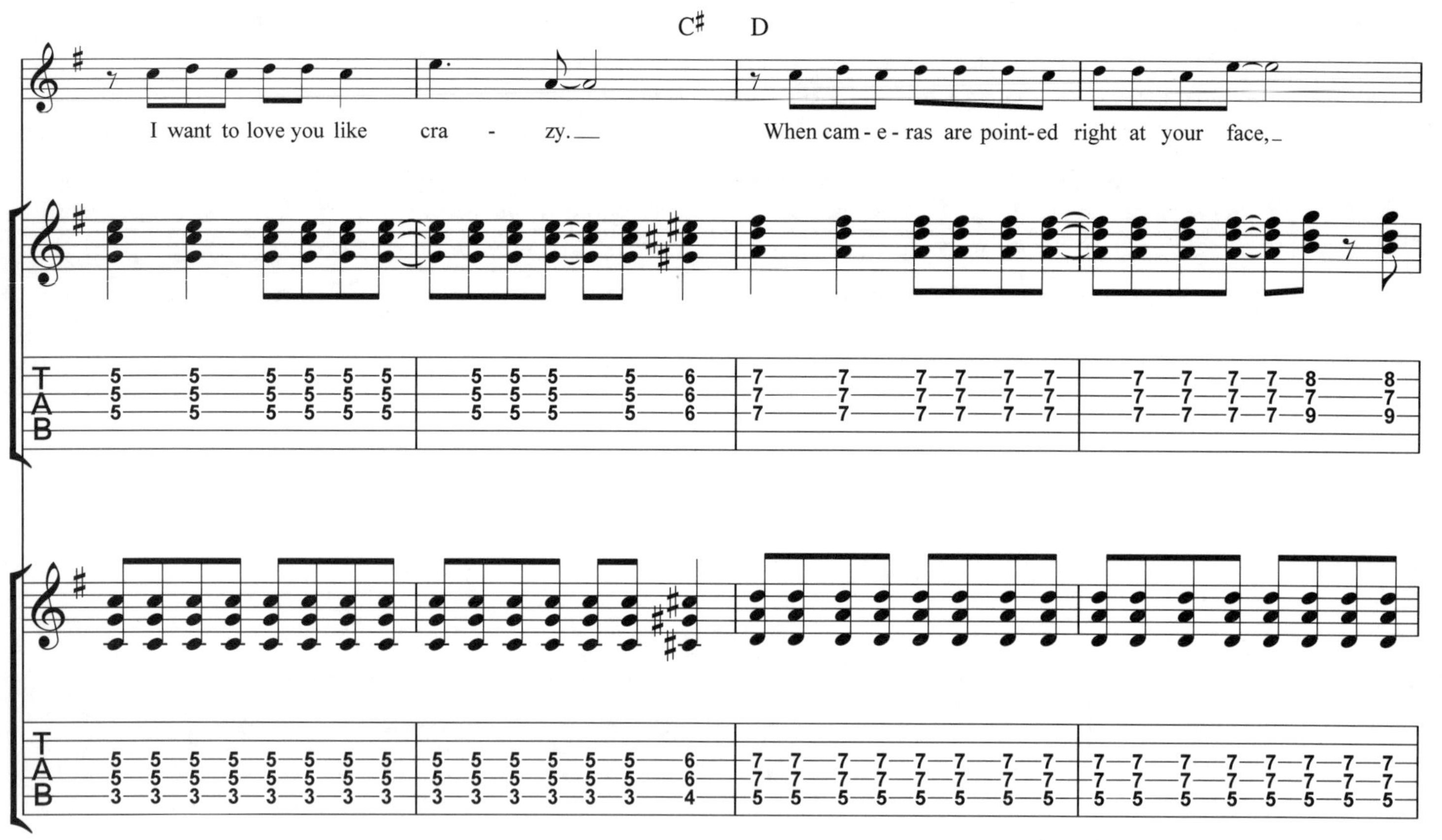

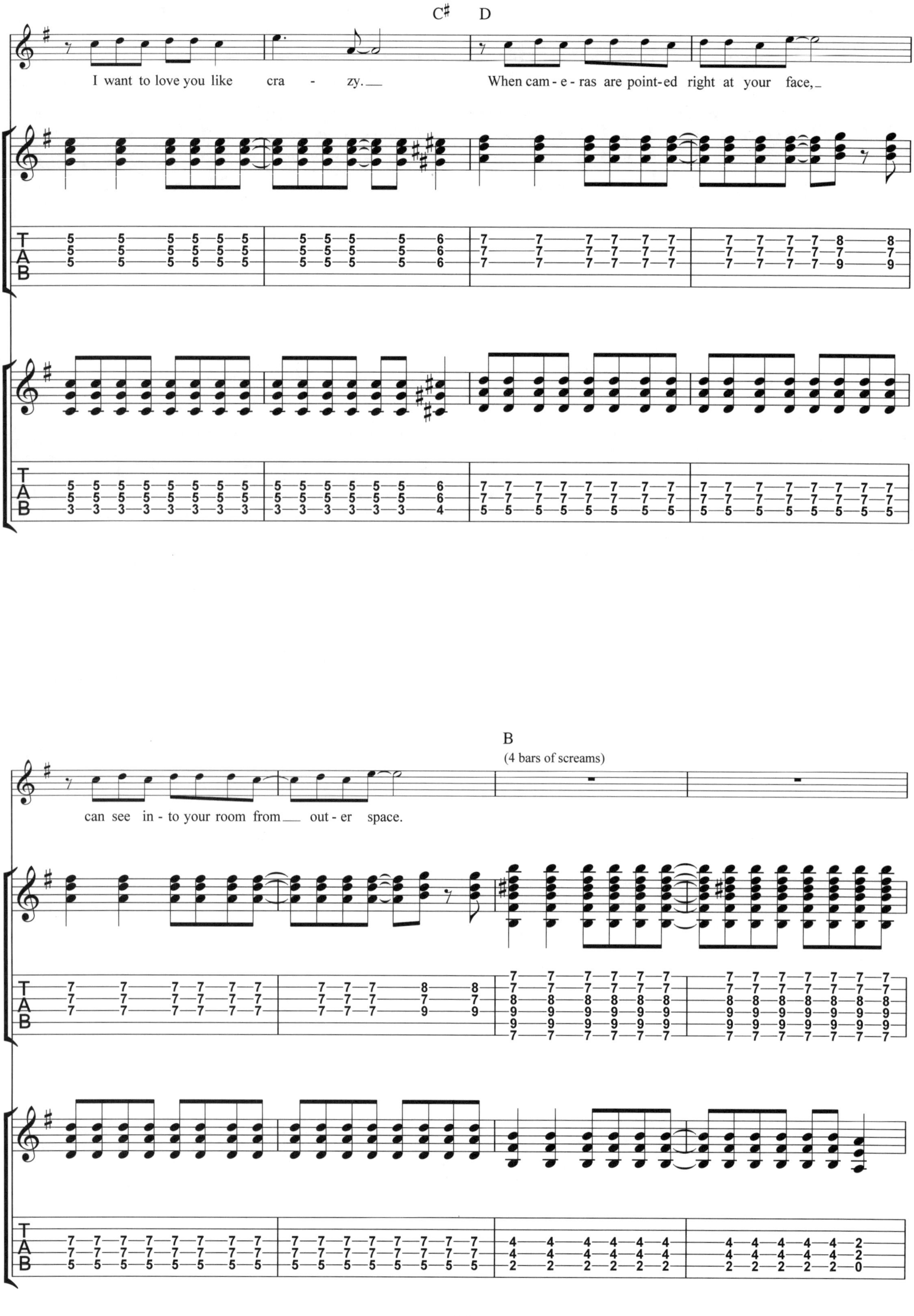

B

(4 bars of screams)

can see in - to your room from out - er space.

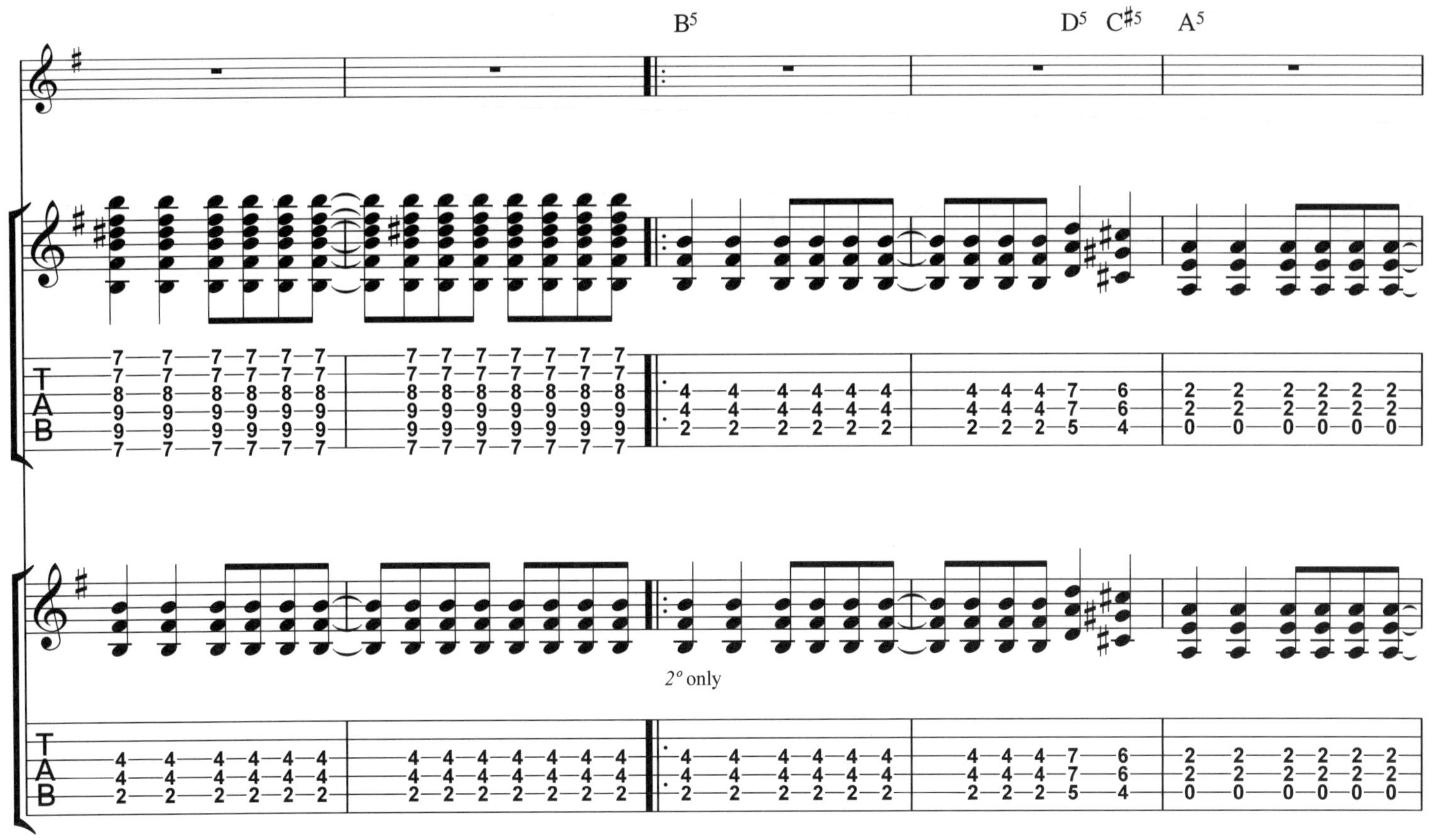
B5
D5 C♯5 A5
2° only

D5 C♯5
C
Oo - wa - oo - wa - oo - wa - oo - wa - oo - wa - oo - wa - oo - wa - oo
oo - wa - oo - wa - oo - wa - oo -

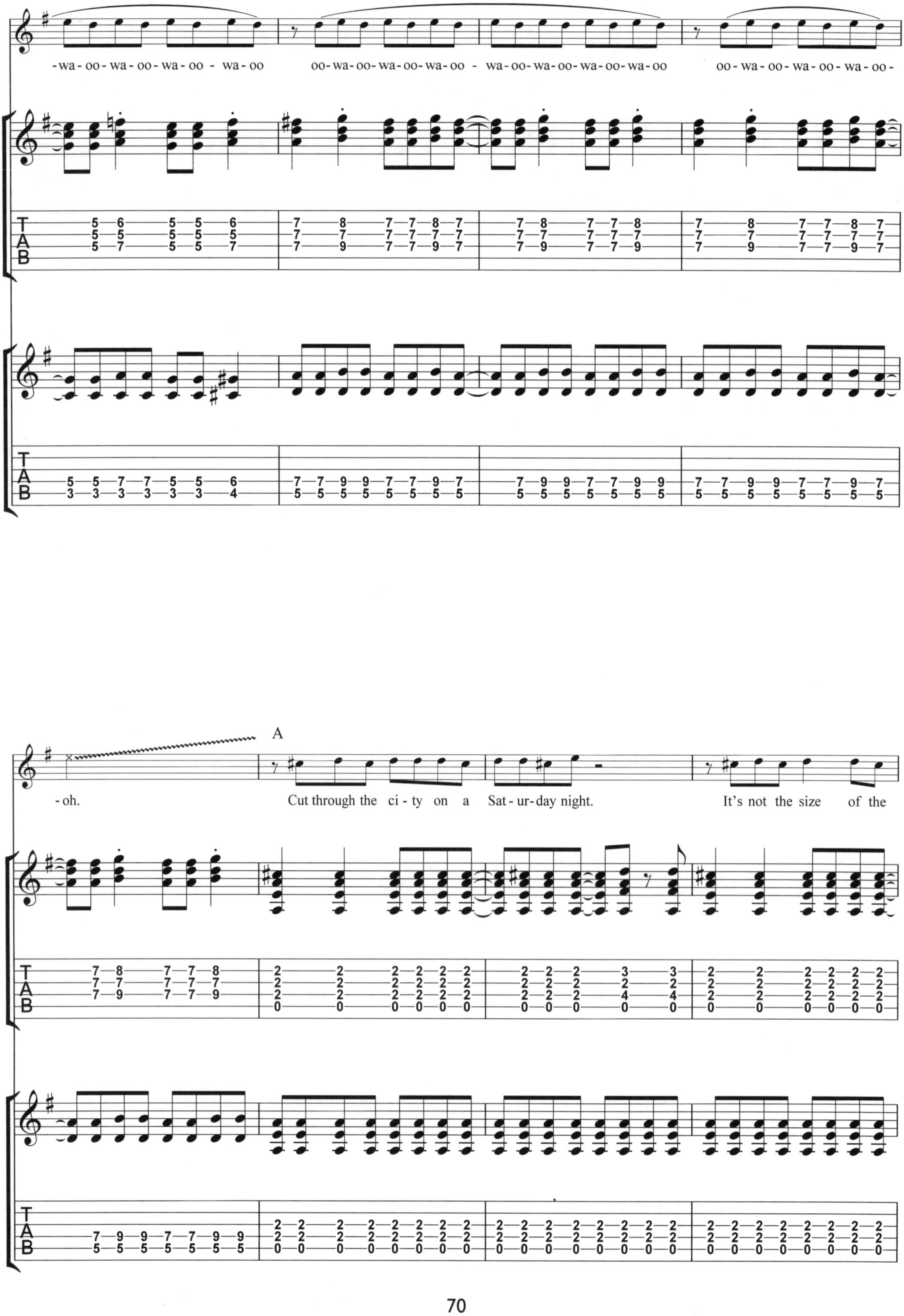

A

- oh. Cut through the ci - ty on a Sat - ur - day night. It's not the size of the

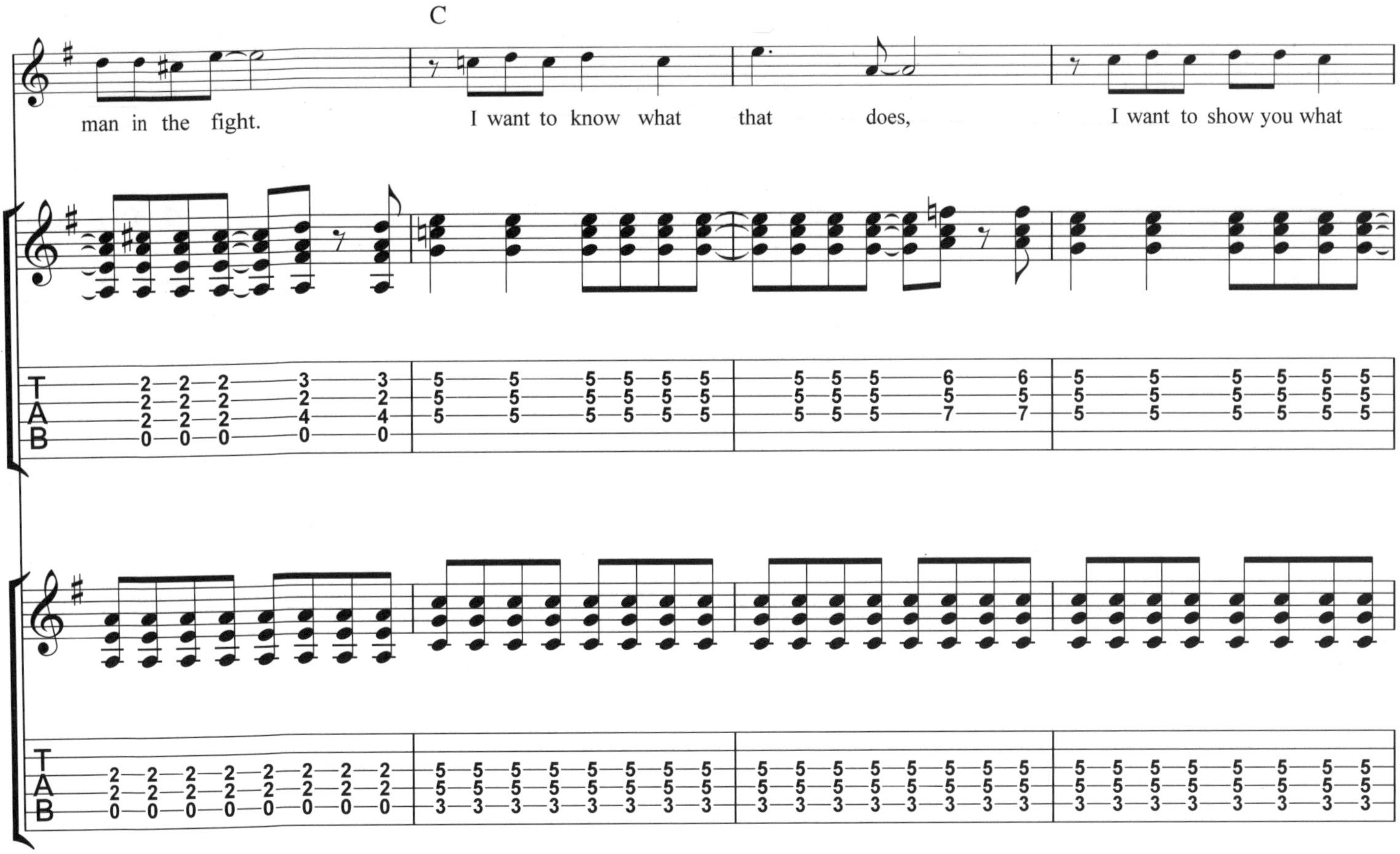

C
man in the fight.
I want to know what that does,
I want to show you what

C♯
D
mat - ters.
'Cos it's the size of the fight in the man.
That makes the differ-ence and de-

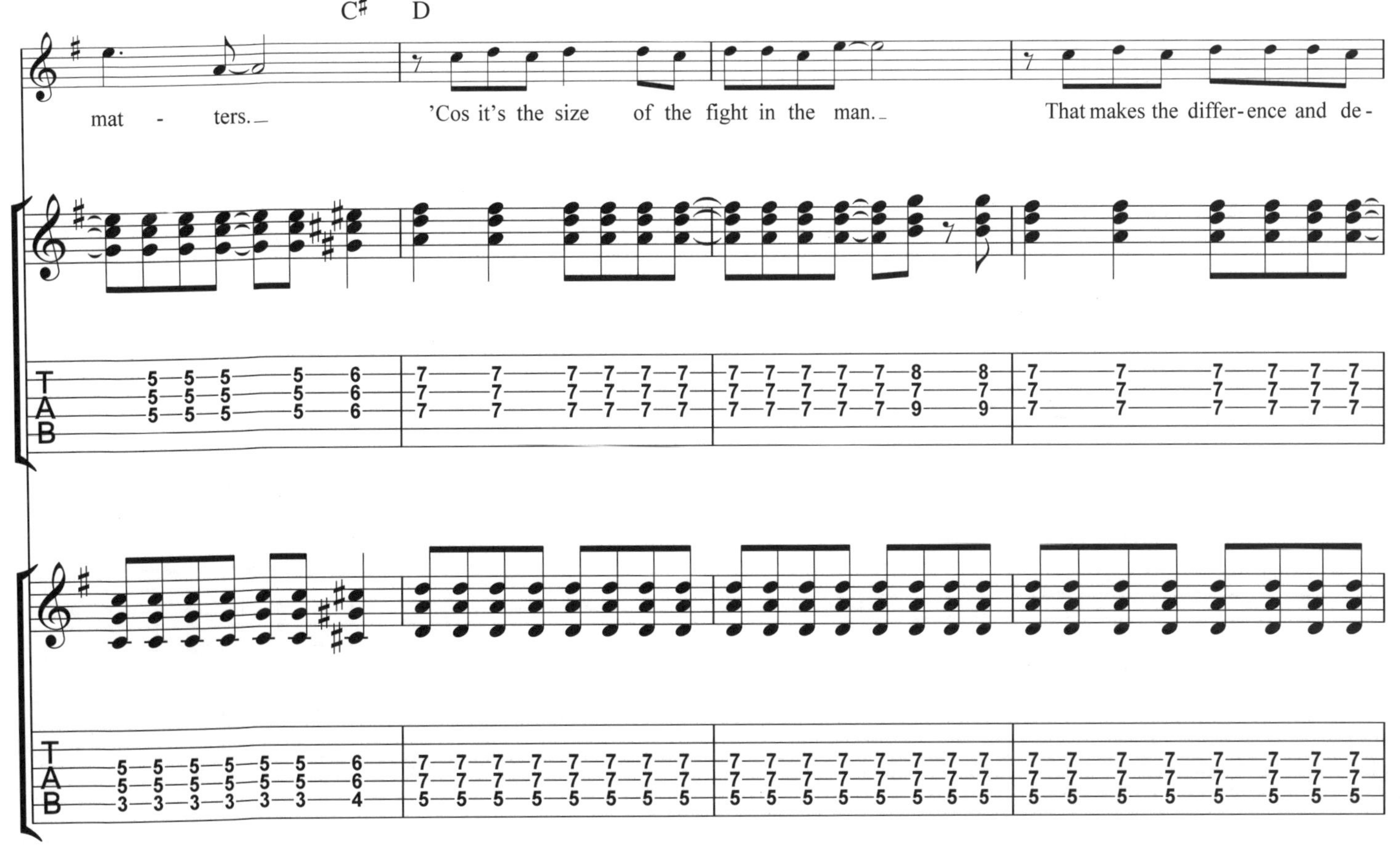

E
-cides who is champ. Cut through the ci - ty on a Sat - ur - day night 'cos you and me__ are on the

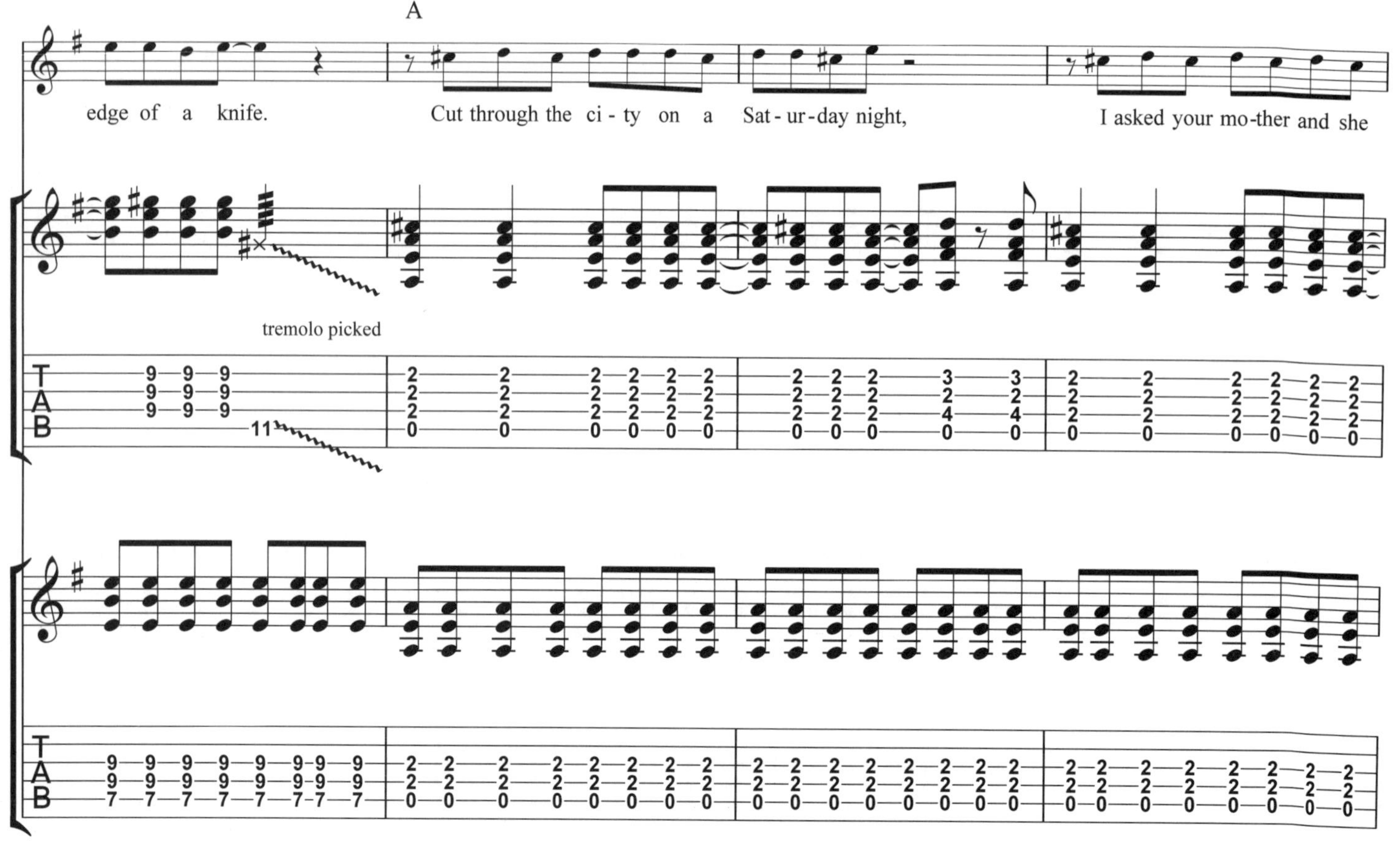
A
edge of a knife. Cut through the ci - ty on a Sat - ur - day night, I asked your mo-ther and she
tremolo picked

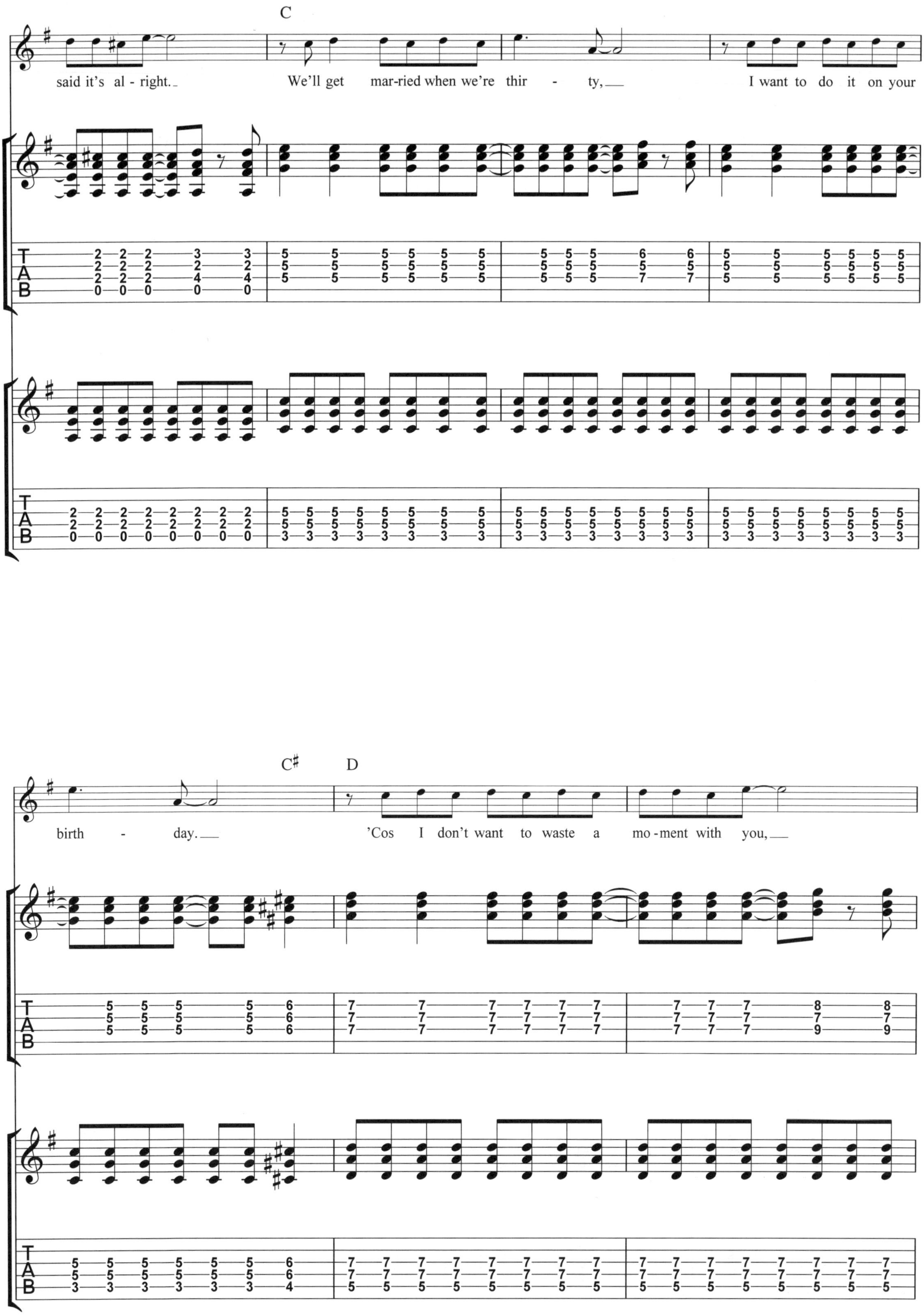

C

said it's al - right.
We'll get mar-ried when we're thir - ty,
I want to do it on your

E
I just want to dance the whole night through.
Cut through the ci - ty on a

A
Sat - ur - day night 'cos you and me__ are on the edge of a knife.
Tapped harmonics*
TA dive*
*arr. from overdubbed Gtr.

What Did I Ever Give You?

Words & Music by Nicholas Hodgson, Richard Wilson, Andrew White, James Rix & Nicholas Baines

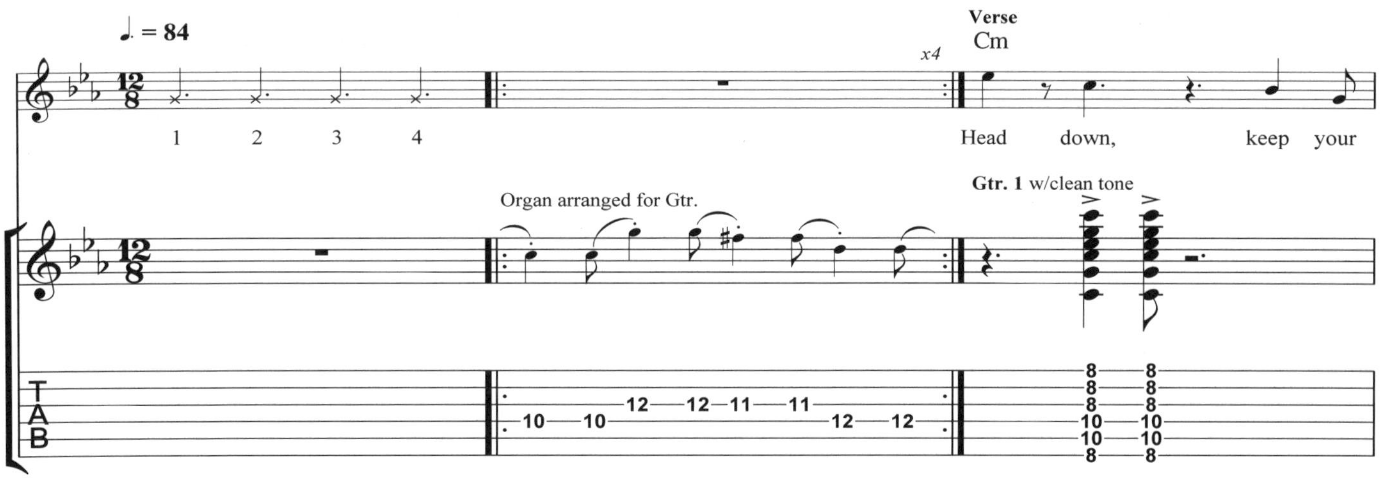

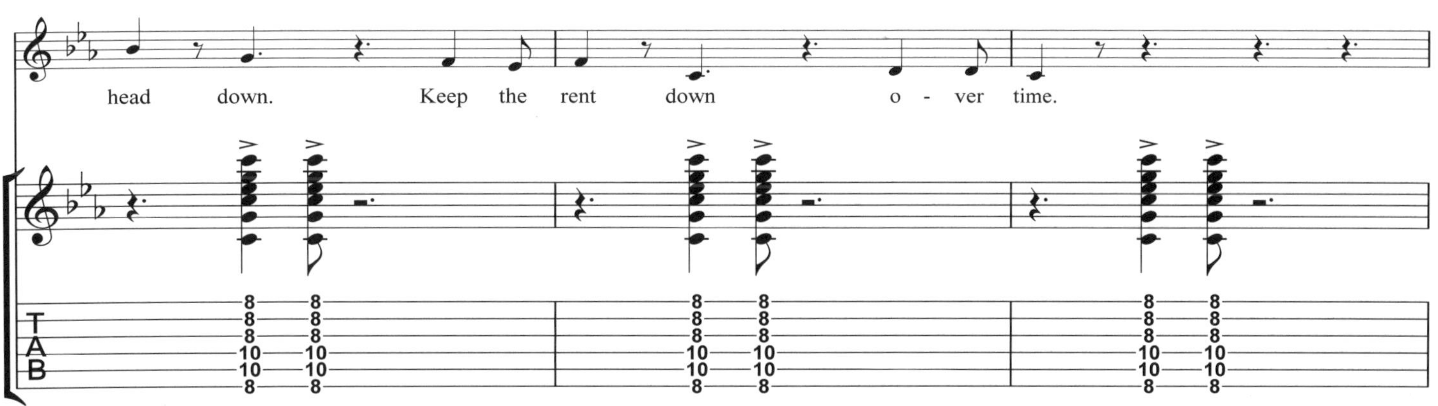

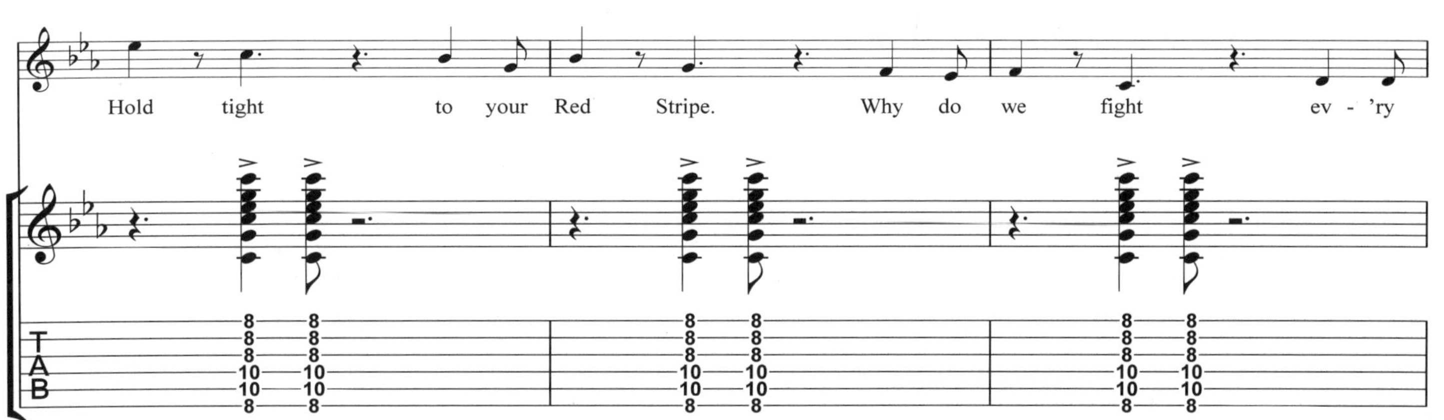

Bridge
B♭
B
time. I wish that you could see me in the day, I
Ah
B♭
Verse
B
Cm
hope that you'll re - mem - ber me that way. Night club, Mal - borough
ah ah ah.
light stub stuck to my gob all the time. I

treat you like you're see through. I don't mean to ev - 'ry

Gtr. 2 w/clean tone

mp

cont. sim.

time. I

Bridge

B♭ B

wish that you could see me in the day, I

ah - - ah - ah - ah

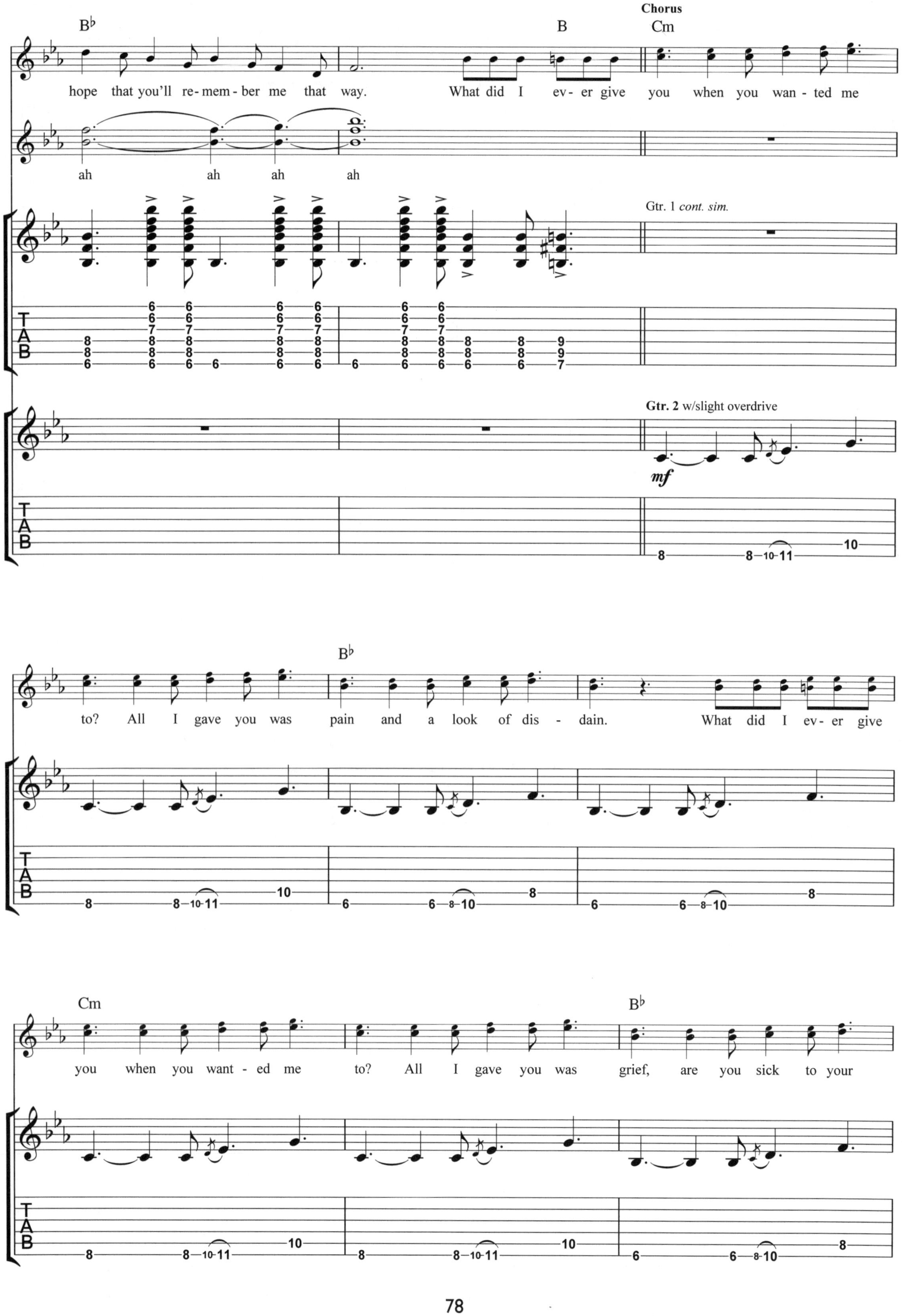

B♭ B Chorus Cm

hope that you'll re-mem-ber me that way. What did I ev-er give you when you wan-ted me

ah ah ah ah

Gtr. 1 *cont. sim.*

Gtr. 2 w/slight overdrive

mf

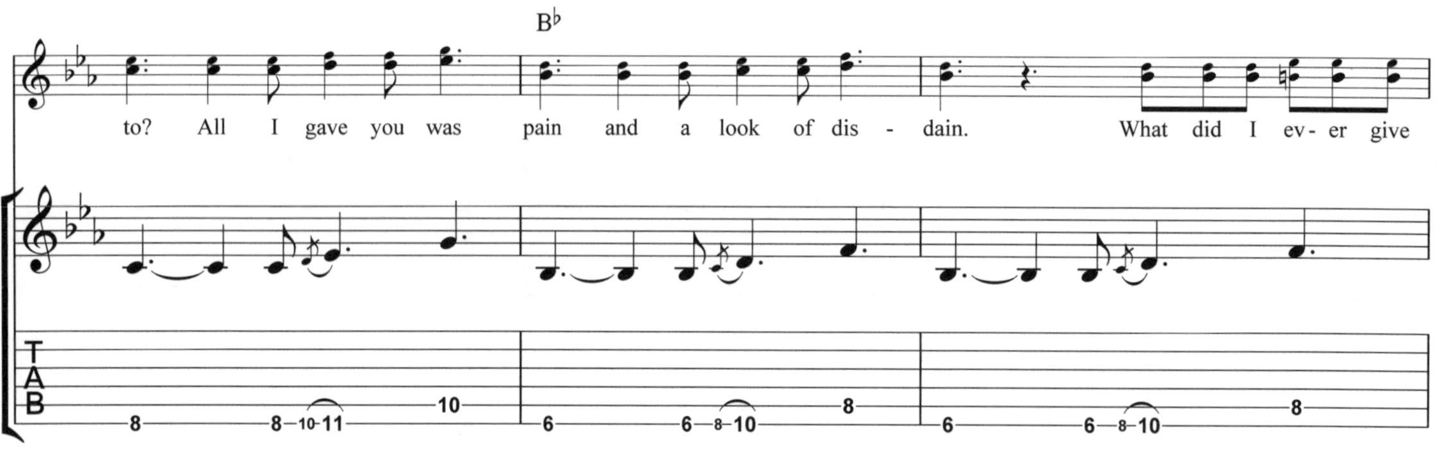

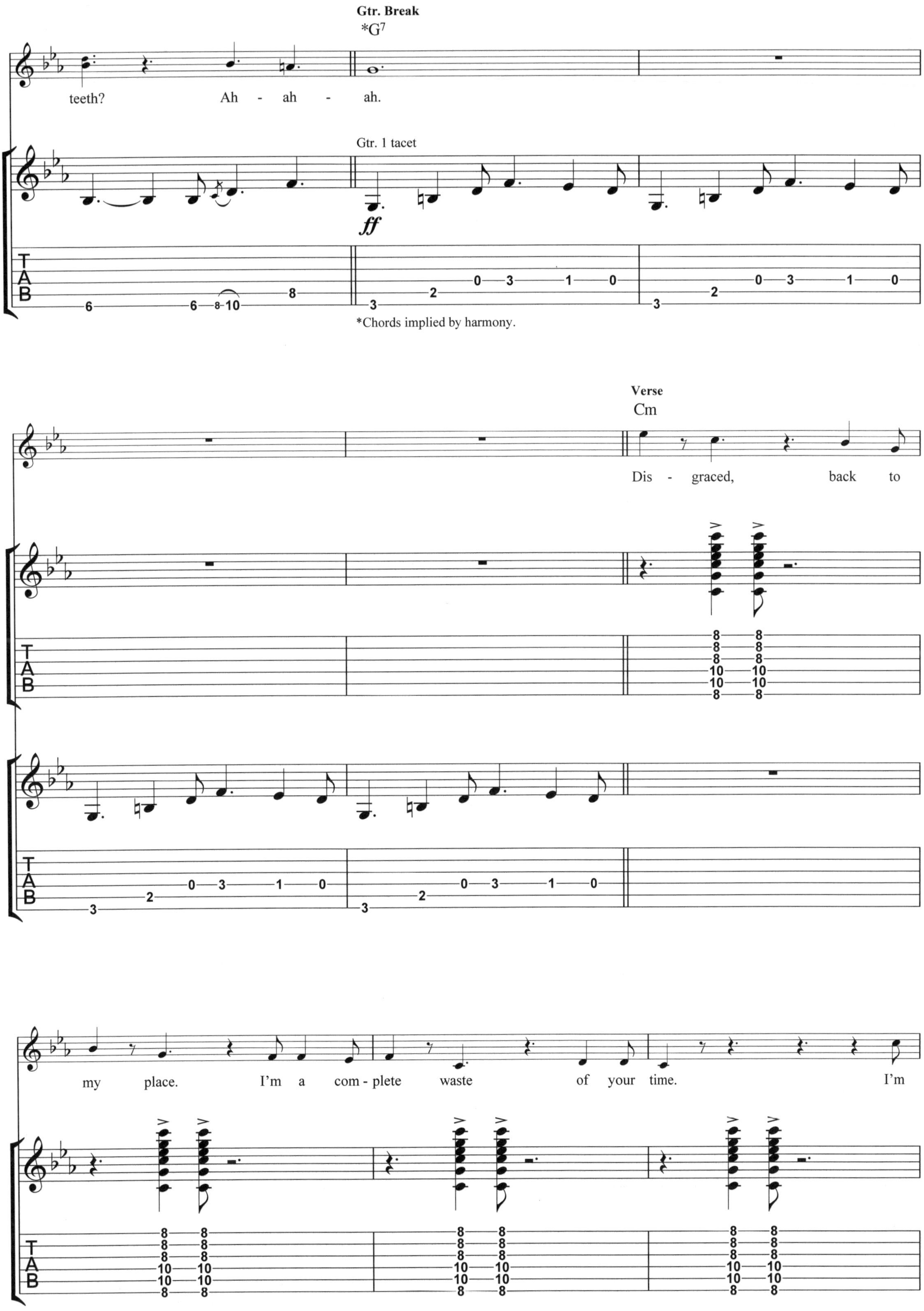

Gtr. Break

*G7

teeth? Ah - ah - ah.

Gtr. 1 tacet

ff

*Chords implied by harmony.

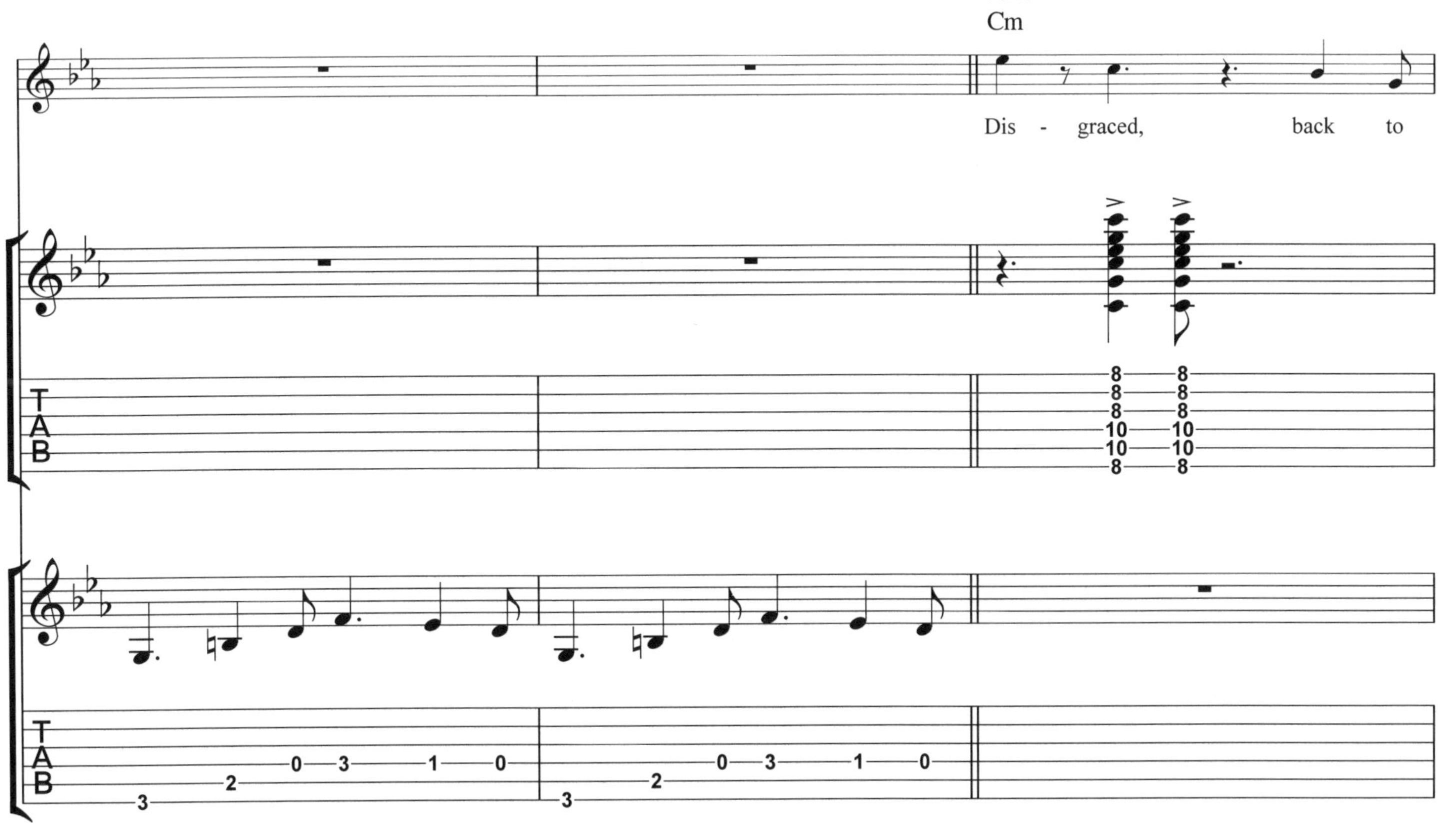

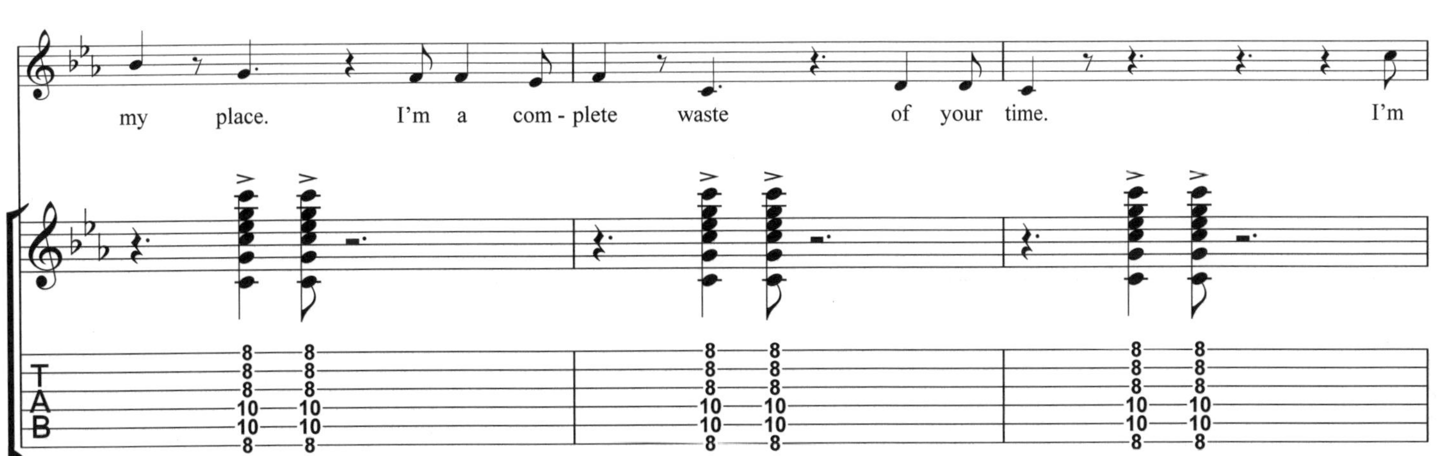

a - sleep be-fore the first sheep, un-til the last bleep of all
Gtr. 2
mp
time. I wish that you could see me in the day, I
Bridge
B♭
B
Ah - ah - ah - ah - ah

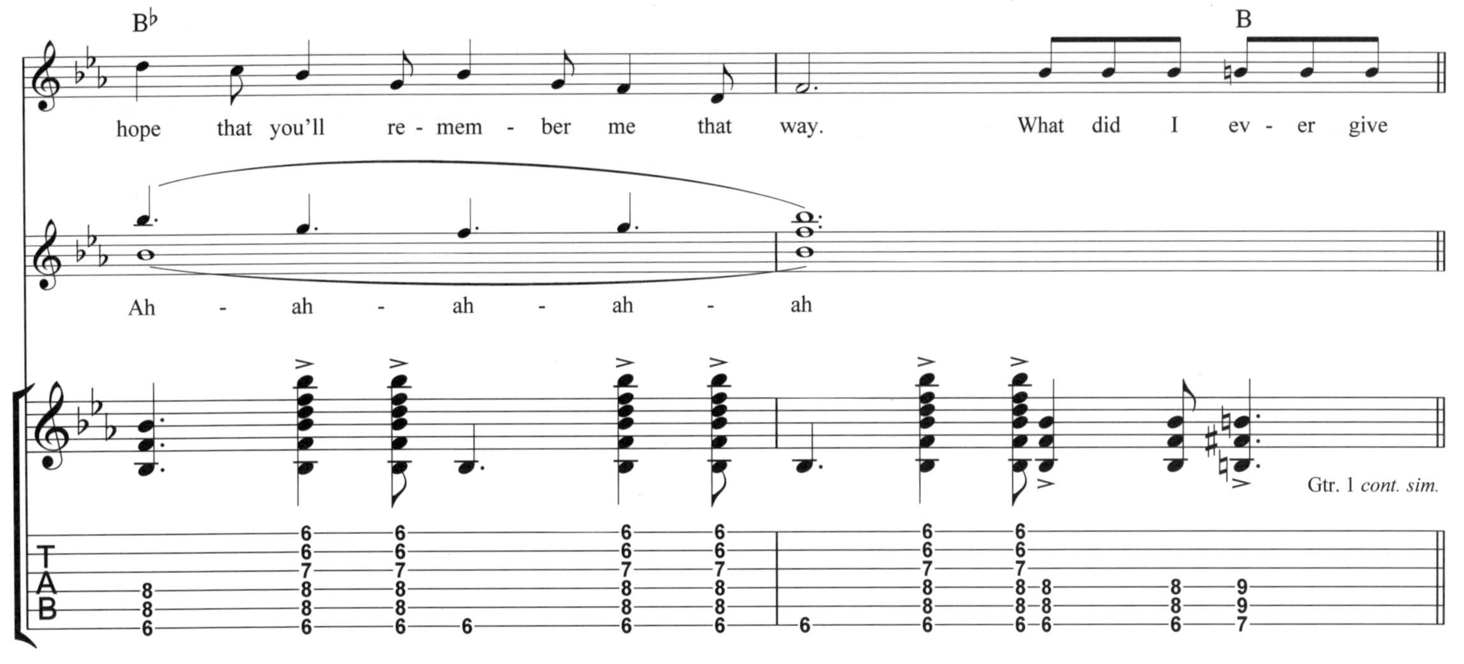
B♭
B
hope that you'll re - mem - ber me that way. What did I ev - er give
Ah - ah - ah - ah - ah
Gtr. 1 cont. sim.

Chorus
Cm
B♭
you when you wan - ted me to? All I gave you was pain and a look of dis -
Gtr. 2 w/slight overdrive
mf

Cm
dain. What did I ev - er give you when you want - ed me to? All I gave you was

Gtr. Break 2
B♭
G
grief. Are you sick to your teeth? Ah - ah - ah.
Gtr. 1 tacet
ff
F
1.
2.
C
C♯
Chorus
Dm
What did I ev - er give you when you wan - ted me
2° only
Ah - - - -
Gtr. 1 cont. sim.
mf

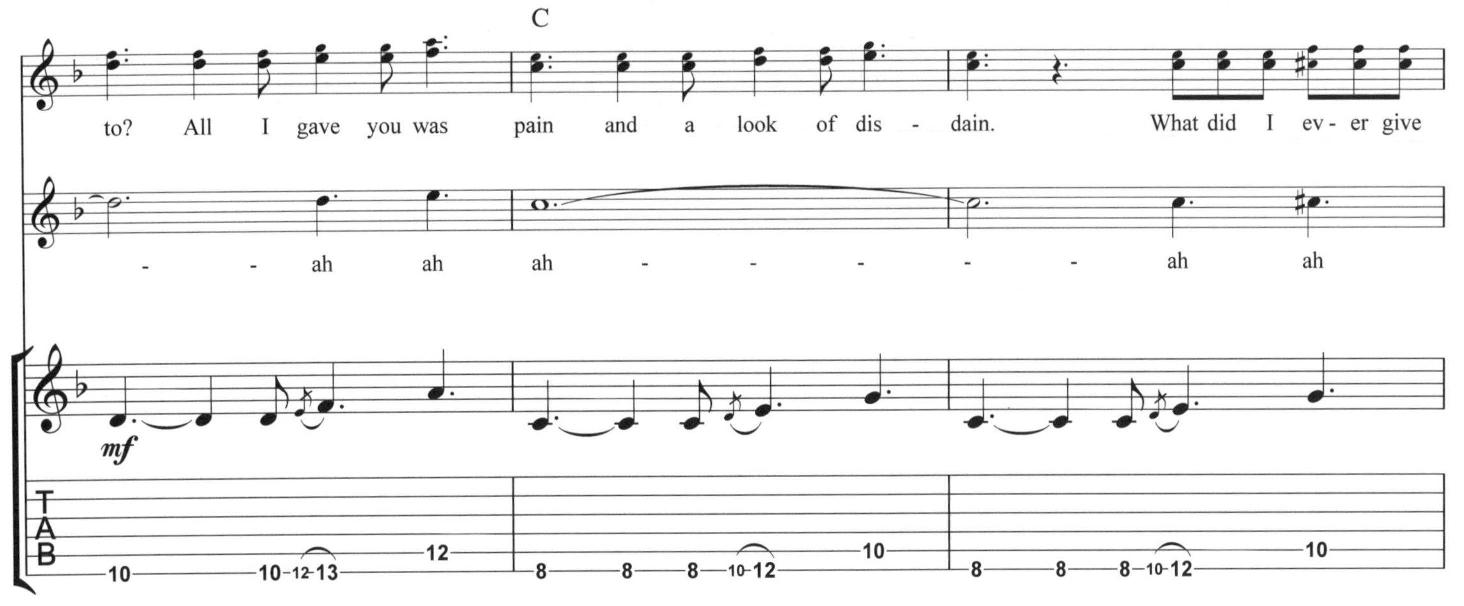
C
to? All I gave you was pain and a look of dis - dain. What did I ev - er give
- - ah ah ah - - - - - ah ah
mf
T
A
B
10 10-12-13 12 8 8 8 10-12 10 8 8 8 10-12 10

Dm
C
you when you want - ed me to? All I gave you was grief, are you sick to your
ah - - - - - - ah ah ah - - -
T
A
B
10 10 10-12-13 12 10 10 10-12-13 12 8 8 8 10-12 10

Dm
teeth? What did I ev - er give you?
1° only
- - ah ah.
T
A
B
8 8 8 10-12 10 10

Time Honoured Tradition

Words & Music by Nicholas Hodgson, Richard Wilson, Andrew White, James Rix & Nicholas Baines

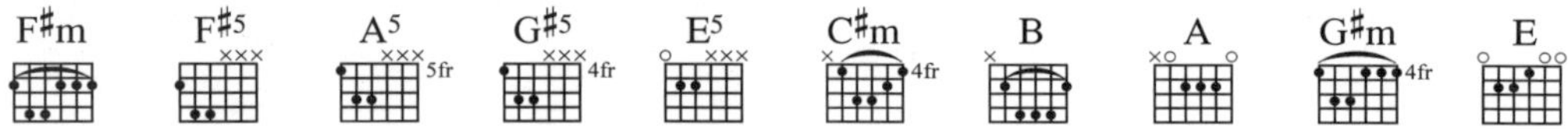

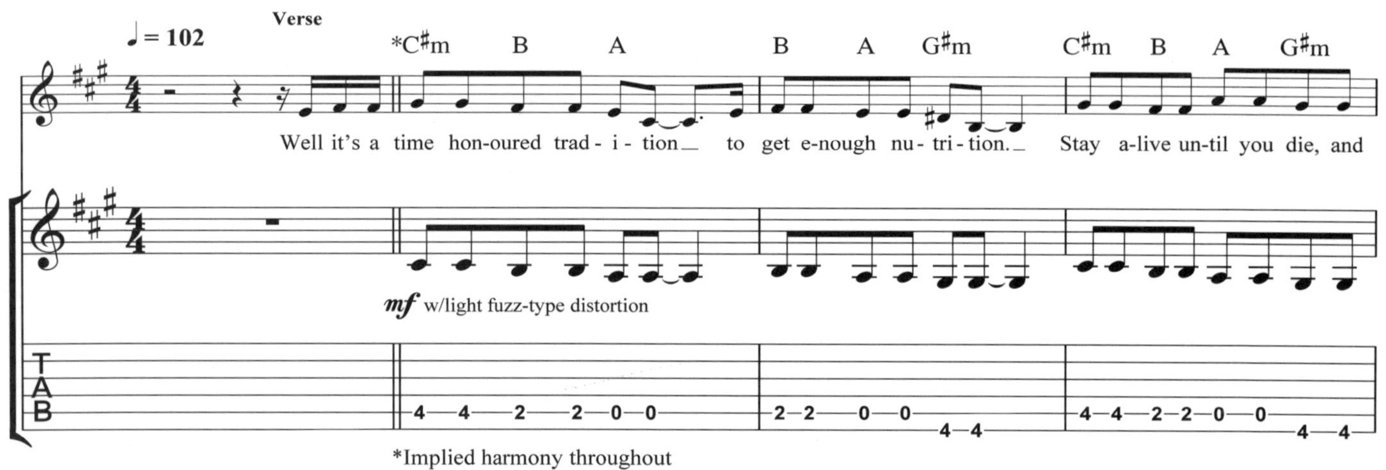

F♯m E F♯m F♯m E F♯m
That is the end of that. That is the end of that.
Bridge
F♯5 A5
Oh oh oh oh
w/dist.
ff
full
f w/dist.
G♯5 A5 G♯5 E5 F♯5 A5 G♯5 A5 G♯5 E5
oh oh oh oh oh oh oh oh oh oh oh oh oh. Well it's
Verse
C♯m B A B A G♯m C♯m B A G♯m
not an old wives tale, too much red meat and ale. Will make you pay get five a day, or
mf w/light fuzz
F♯m E F♯m C♯m B A B A G♯m
that is the end of you. And it's a com-mon mis-con-cep-tion, but true, with-out ex-cep-tion. These

C♯m B A G♯m F♯m E F♯m F♯m E F♯m
nights of booze catch up with yous. And that is an ac - tu - al fact. That is the end of that.

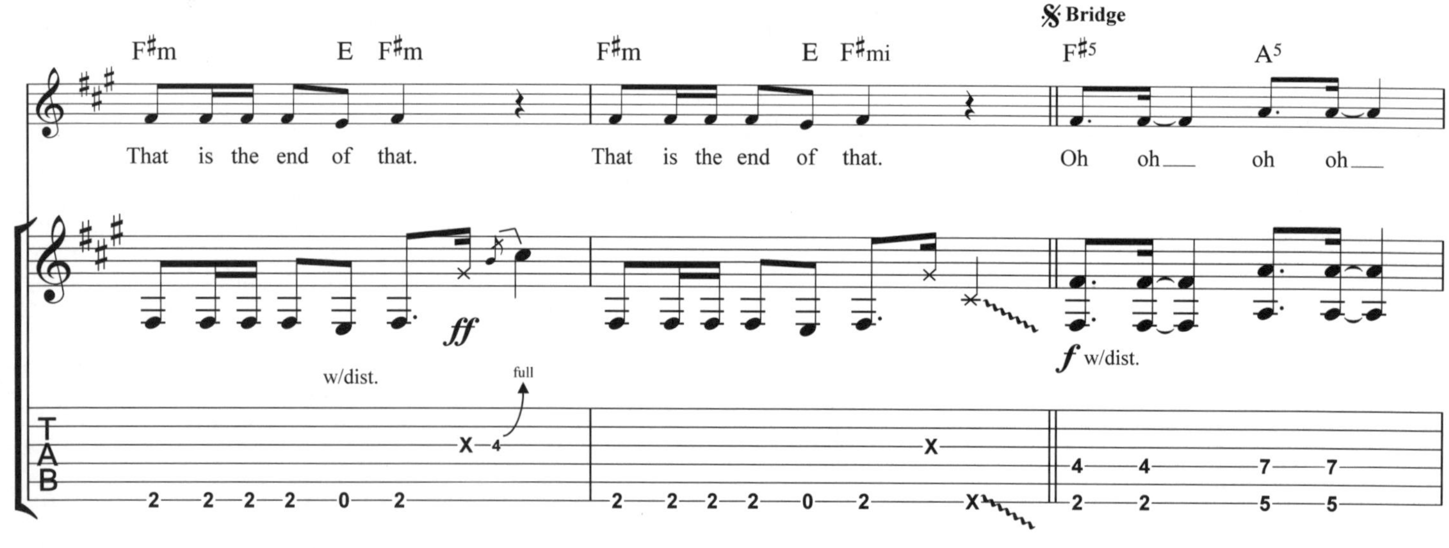
Bridge
F♯m E F♯m F♯m E F♯mi F♯5 A5
That is the end of that. That is the end of that. Oh oh oh oh
ff
w/dist.
full
f w/dist.

G♯5 A5 G♯5 E5 F♯5 A5 G♯5 A5 G♯5 E5
oh oh oh oh oh oh oh oh oh oh oh oh oh

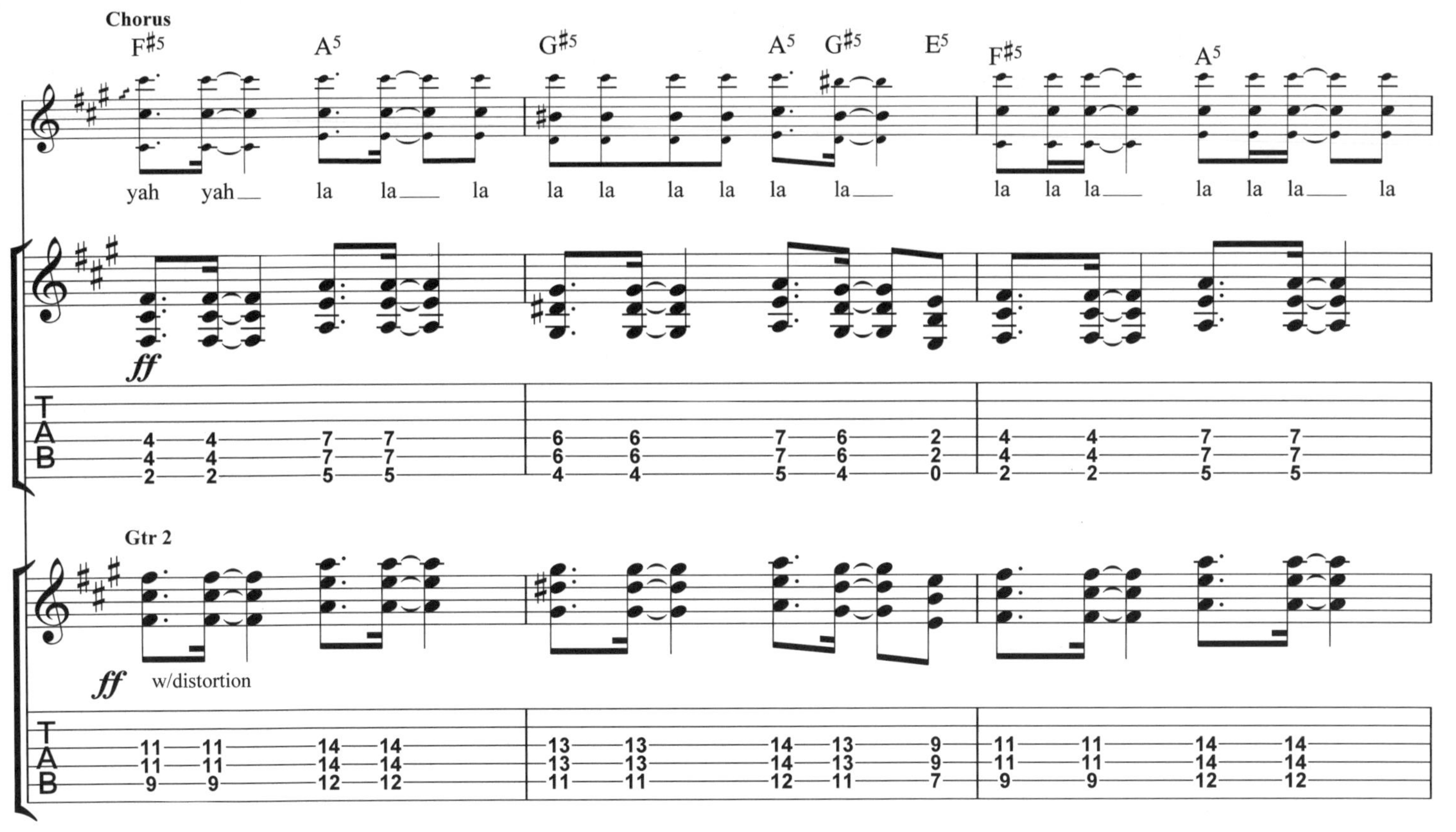

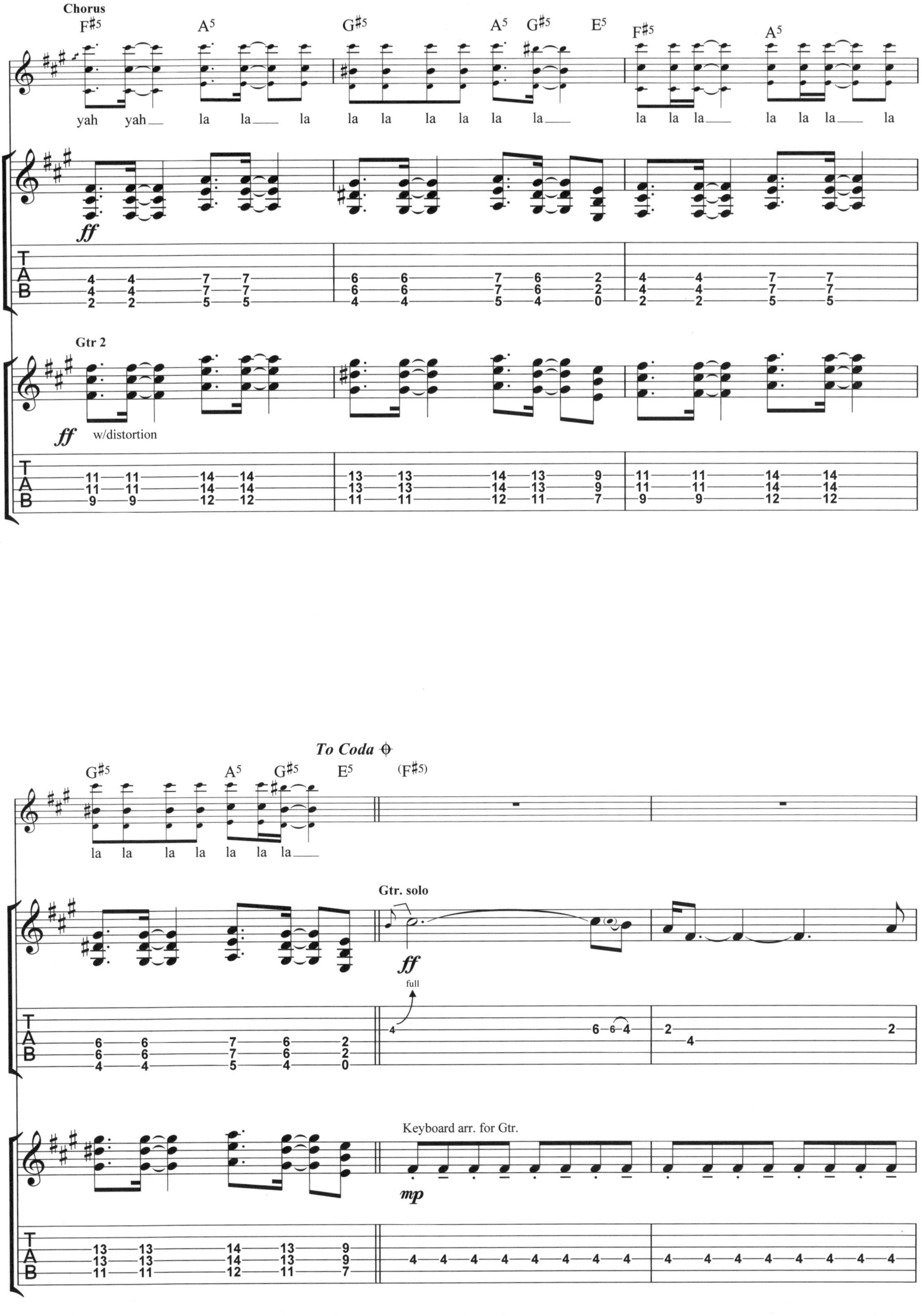

To Coda

G♯5 A5 G♯5 E5 (F♯5)

la la la la la la la

Gtr. solo

ff

full

Keyboard arr. for Gtr.

mp

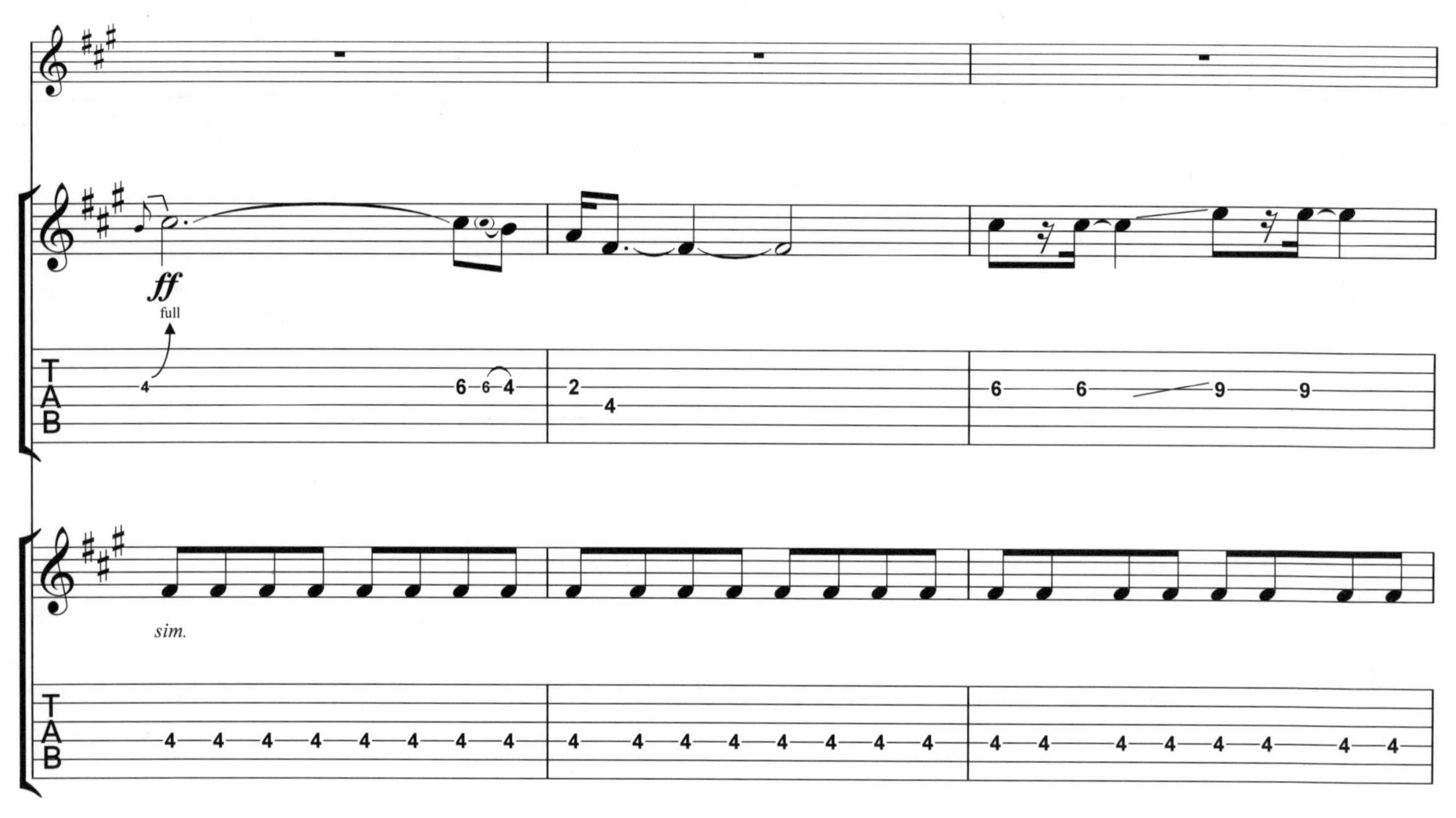
ff
full
sim.
T
A
B
T
A
B

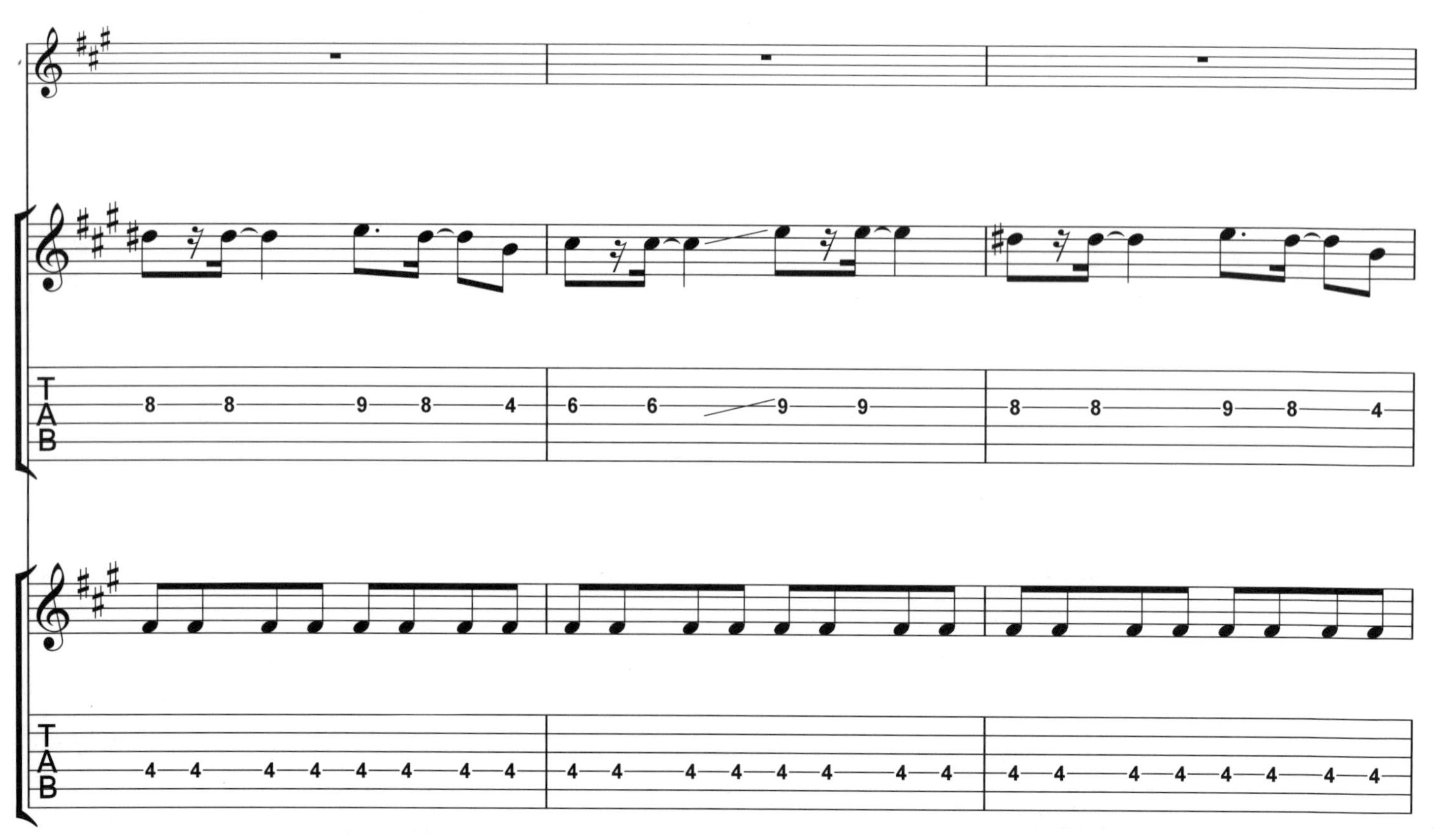
T
A
B
T
A
B

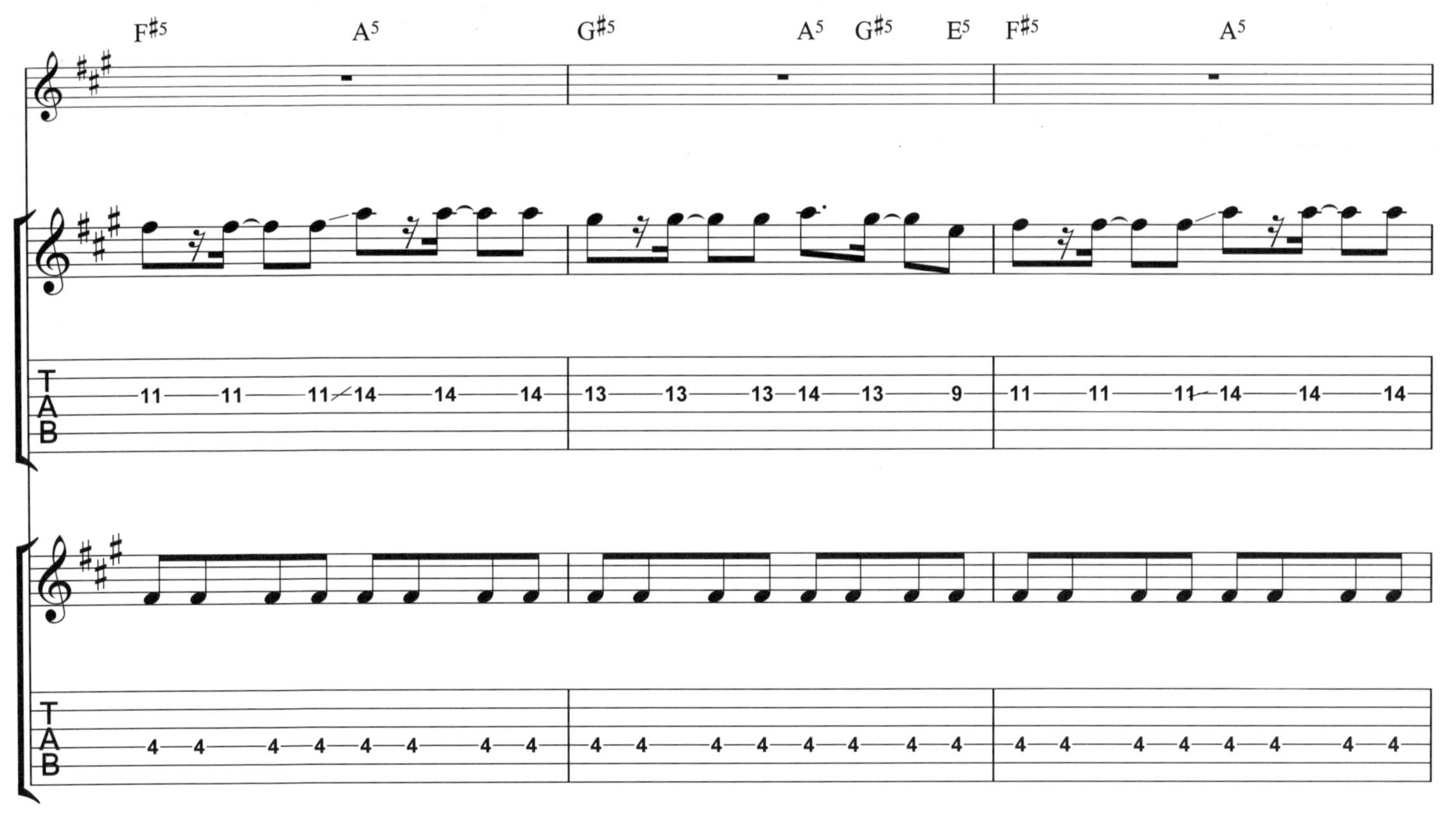
F♯5
A5
G♯5
A5
G♯5
E5
F♯5
A5

G♯5
A5
G♯5
E5
Interlude
F♯5
A5
G♯5
A5
G♯5
E5

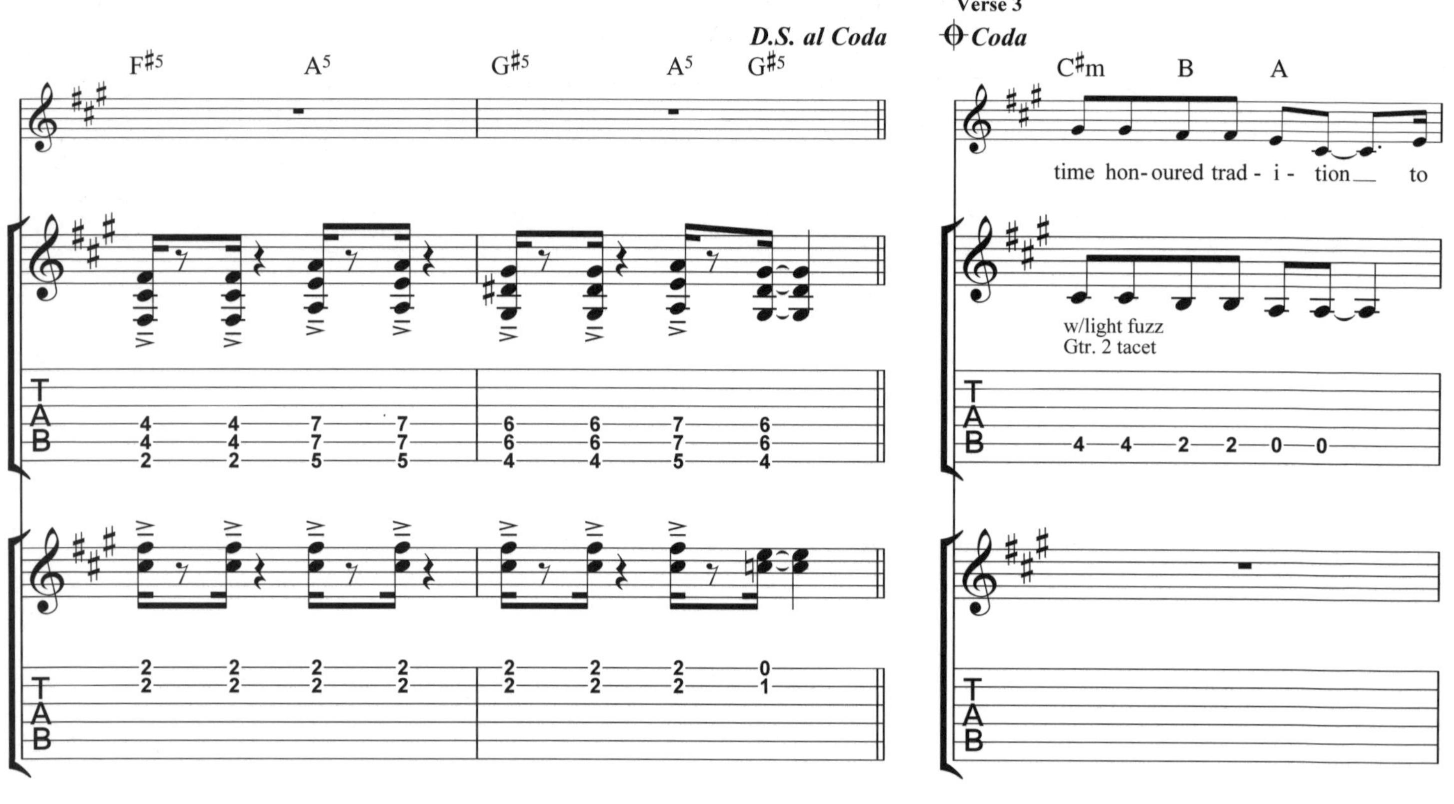
D.S. al Coda
Verse 3
Coda
F#5
A5
G#5
A5
G#5
C#m
B
A
time hon-oured trad - i - tion to
w/light fuzz
Gtr. 2 tacet
T
A
B
4 4 7 7 6 6 7 6
4 4 7 7 6 6 7 6
2 2 5 5 4 4 5 4
4 4 2 2 0 0
2 2 2 2 2 2 2 0
2 2 2 2 2 2 2 1

B
A
G#m
C#m
B
A
G#m
F#m
E F#m
C#m
B
A
get e-nough nu- tri - tion. Stay a-live un- til you die and that is the end of you. And I pi - ty the fools who
T
A
B
2 2 0 0 4 4
4 4 2 2 0 0 4 4
2 2 2 2 0 2
4 4 2 2 0 0

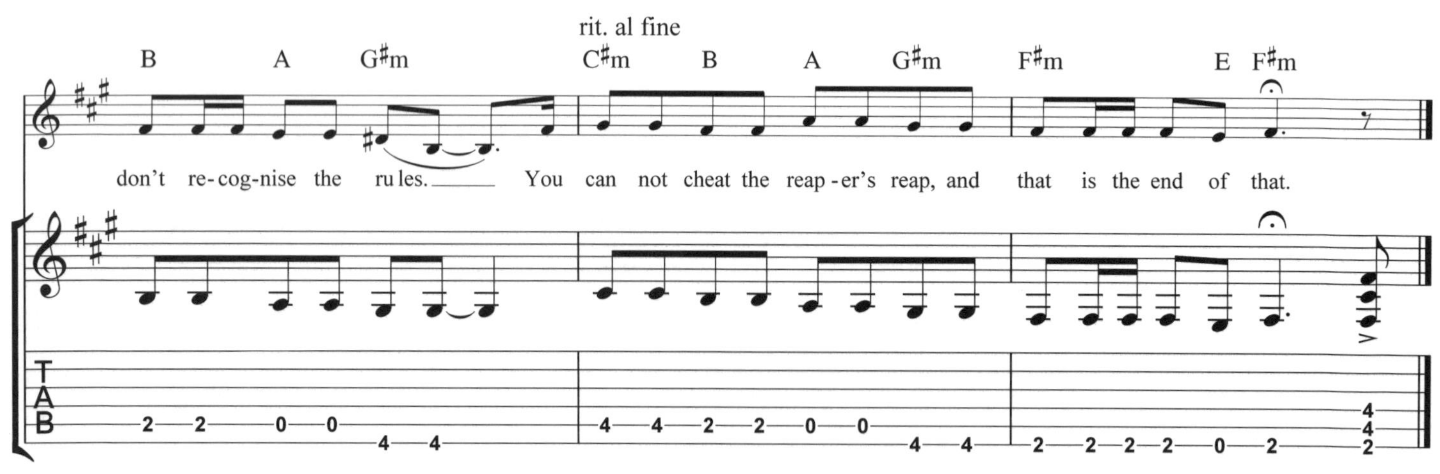
rit. al fine
B
A
G#m
C#m
B
A
G#m
F#m
E
F#m
don't re-cog-nise the ru les. You can not cheat the reap - er's reap, and that is the end of that.
T
A
B
2 2 0 0 4 4
4 4 2 2 0 0 4 4
2 2 2 2 0 2
4 4 2

Caroline, Yes

Words & Music by Nicholas Hodgson, Richard Wilson,
Andrew White, James Rix & Nicholas Baines

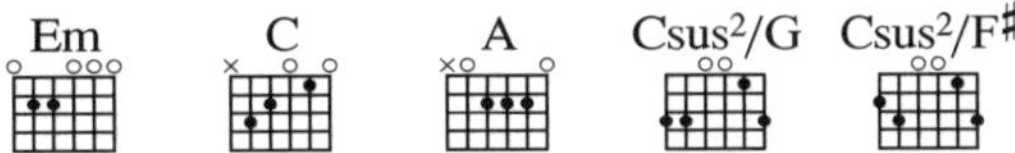

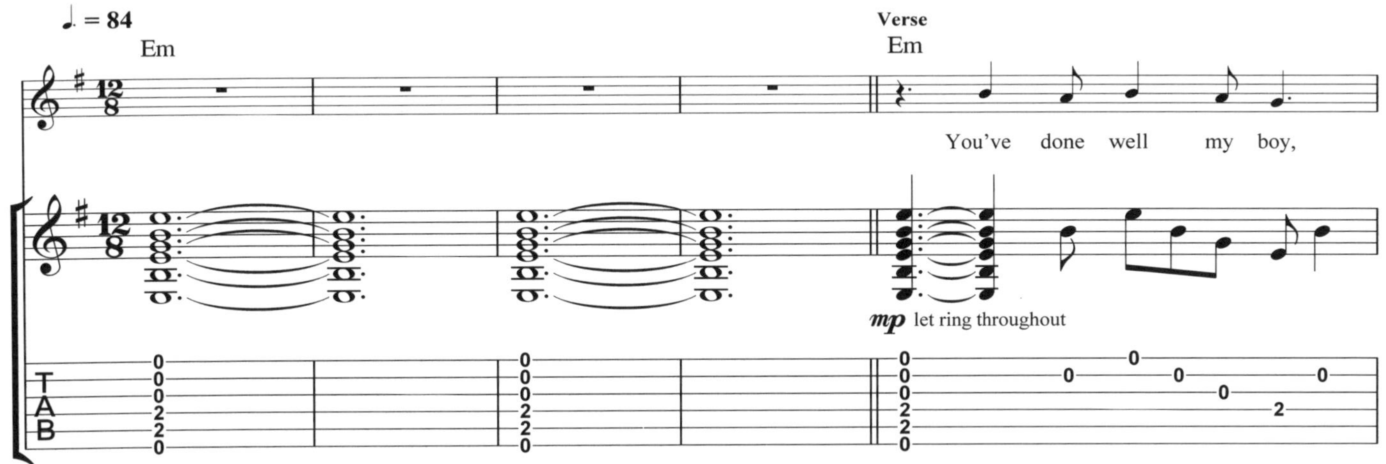

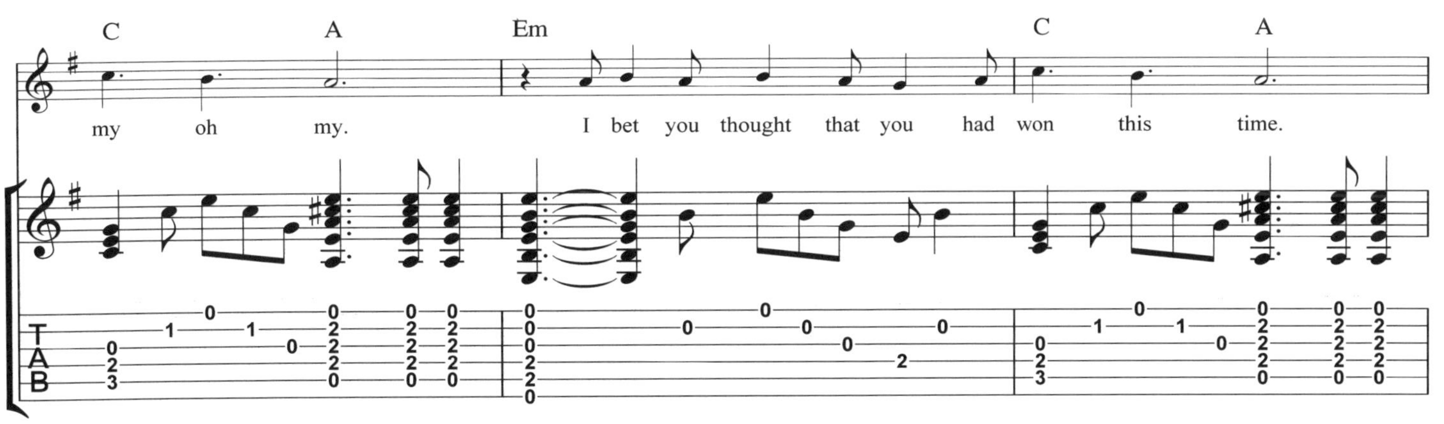

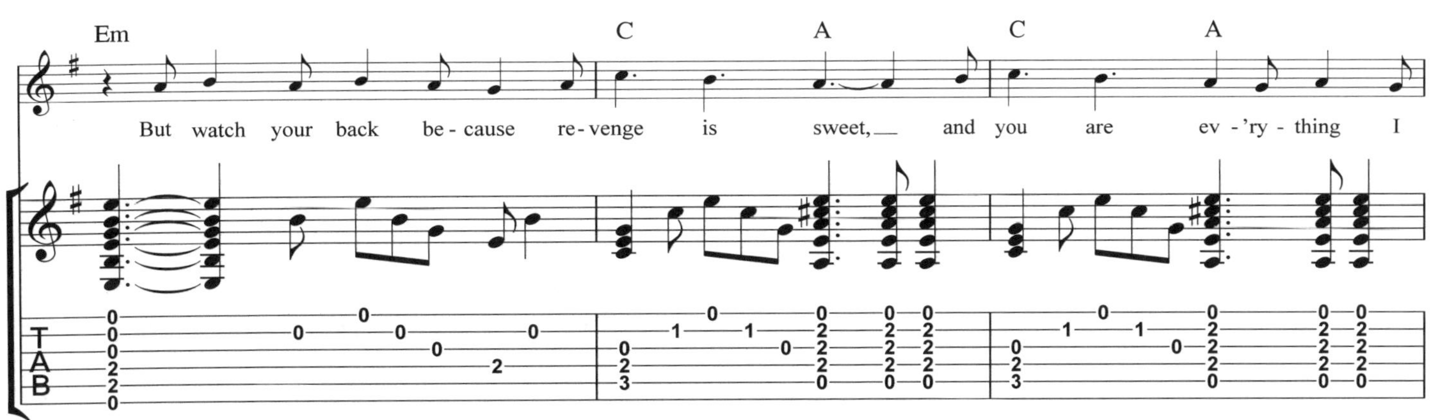

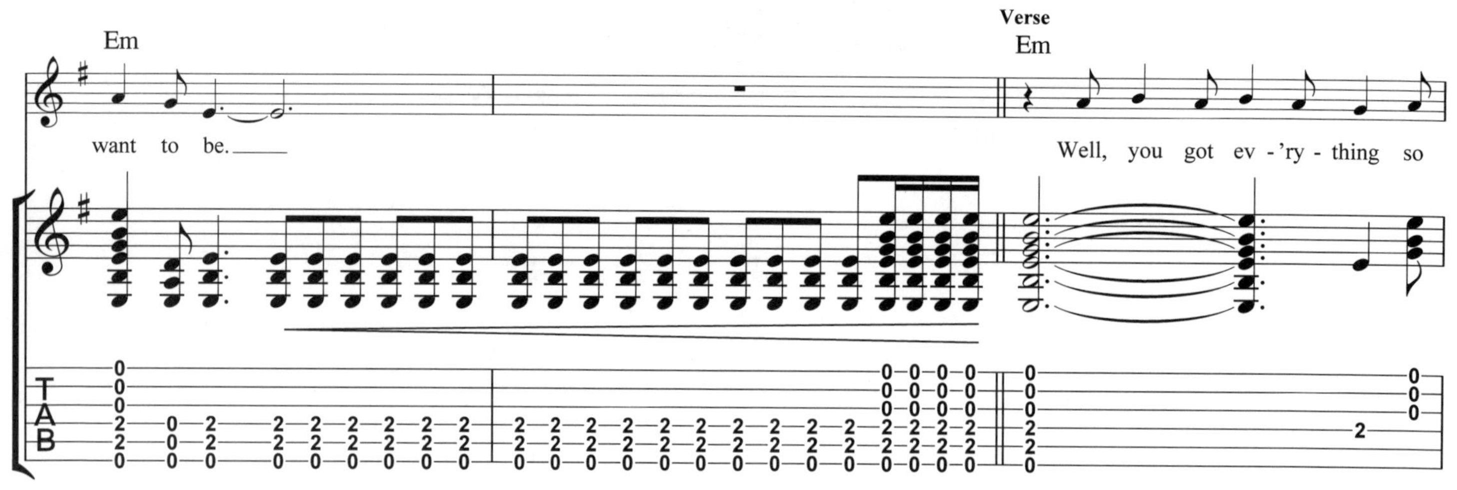
Em
want to be.
Verse
Em
Well, you got ev - 'ry - thing so
T
A
B

C A Em C A
why, oh why, did you have to take Car - o - line?
Ah ah ah ah ah
T
A
B

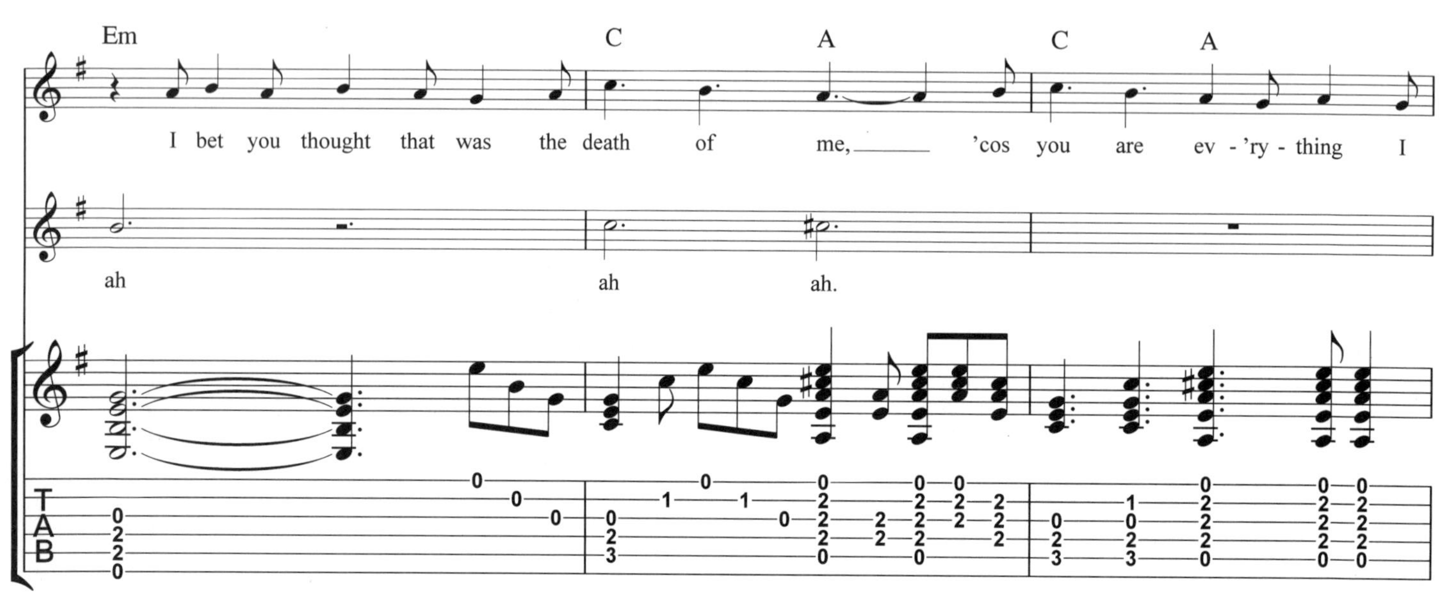
Em C A C A
I bet you thought that was the death of me, 'cos you are ev - 'ry - thing I
ah ah ah.
T
A
B

Chorus
Em
A
want to be.
In my
life.
Ah
gradually increase gain
w/overdrive
Csus2/G
(Csus2/F♯)
Em
In my
ah
oo - oo - oo - oo - oo - oo - oo
oo - oo - oo - oo - oo - oo - oo
1/4
A
Csus2/G
Csus2/F♯
Em
life.
ah
(life)
oo - oo - oo - oo - oo - oo - oo
1/4

Verse
Em
C
A
Well you go your way and I'll go mine.
oo-oo - oo-oo - oo-oo - oo.
Ah ah
full
w/clean tone (overdrive off)
T
A
B
Em
C
A
Em
But my way's bet - ter and it took less time.
Peop - le say now that you
ah ah ah ah
C
A
C
A
Em
look like me, 'cos you are ev - 'ry - thing I want to be.
ah ah.
gradually increase gain

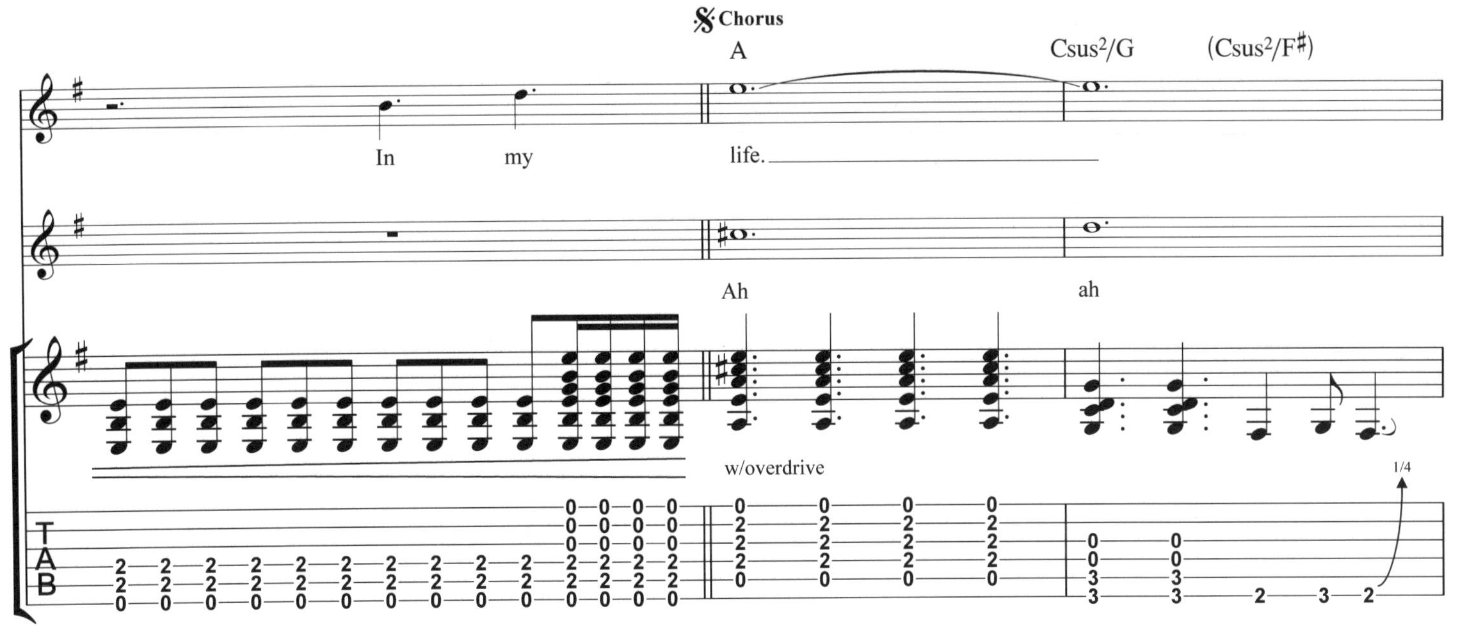
Chorus
A
Csus2/G
(Csus2/F♯)
In
my
life.
Ah
ah
w/overdrive
1/4

Em
A
In
my
life.
oo - oo - oo - oo - oo - oo - oo
oo - oo - oo - oo - oo - oo - oo
ah
(life)

Csus2/G
(Csus2/F♯)
Em
To Coda
In
my
oo - oo - oo - oo - oo - oo - oo
oo - oo - oo - oo - oo - oo - oo
1/4
full

A
Csus2/G
Csus2/F♯
life.
ah
(life)
ff
Em
C
A
Em
C
A
Guitar solo
Em
C
A
C
A
Em
mf
1/4

Em
C
A
Ah
ah
ff
1/4
T
A
B
Em
C
A
Em
C
A
'Cos
ah
ah
ah
ah
ah
ah
'cos
C
A
Em
D.S. al Coda
you are ev - 'ry - thing I want to be.
In my
you are ev - 'ry - thing I want to be.
f
1/4

Coda
Chorus
A
Csus2/G
(Csus2/F♯)
Em
life.
ah.
Oo - oo - oo - oo - oo - oo - oo
1/4
A
Csus2/G
(Csus2/F♯)
In my life.
oo - oo - oo - oo - oo - oo - oo ah (life)
1/4
(Piano)

Team Mate

Words & Music by Nicholas Hodgson, Richard Wilson,
Andrew White, James Rix & Nicholas Baines

G
E
C
D
F♯m
A

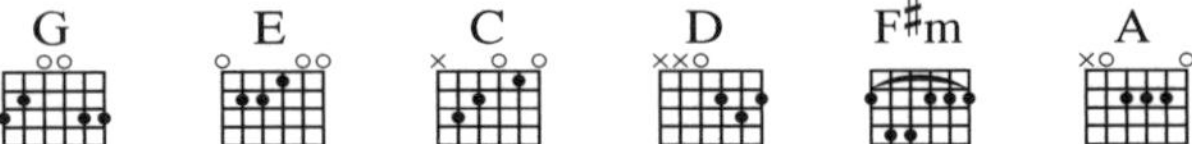

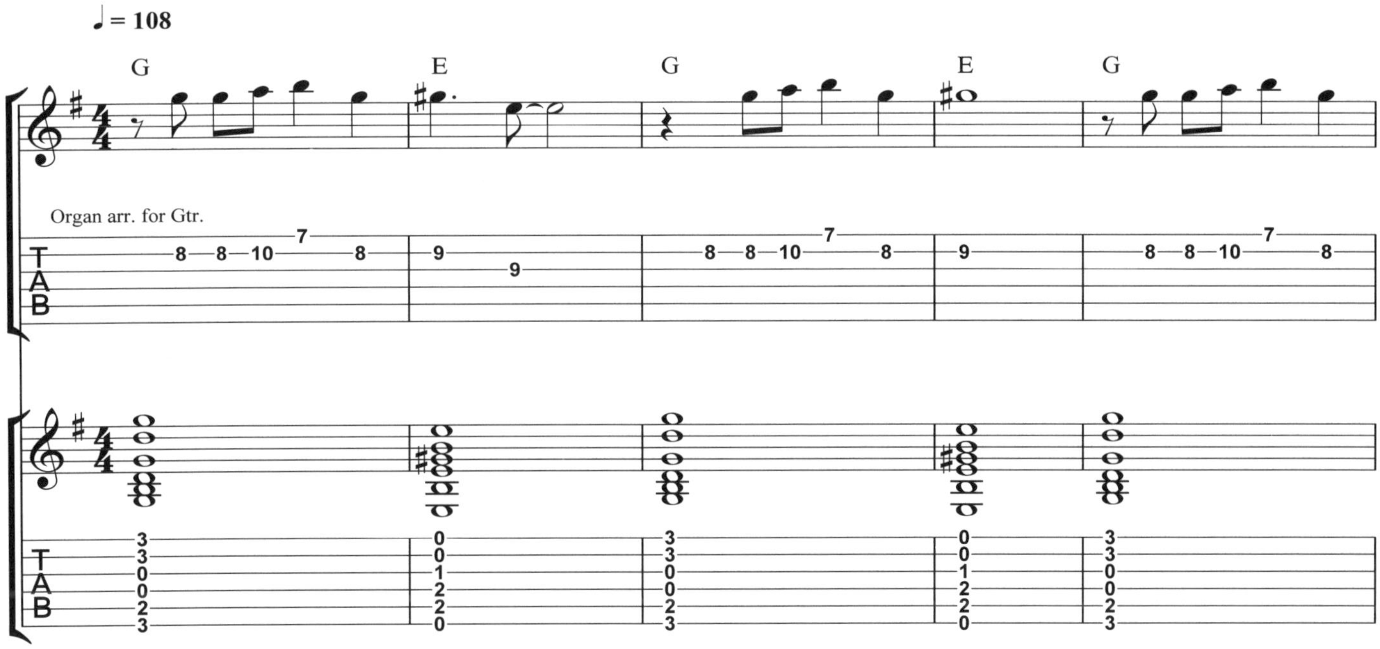

♩ = 108
G
E
G
E
G
Organ arr. for Gtr.

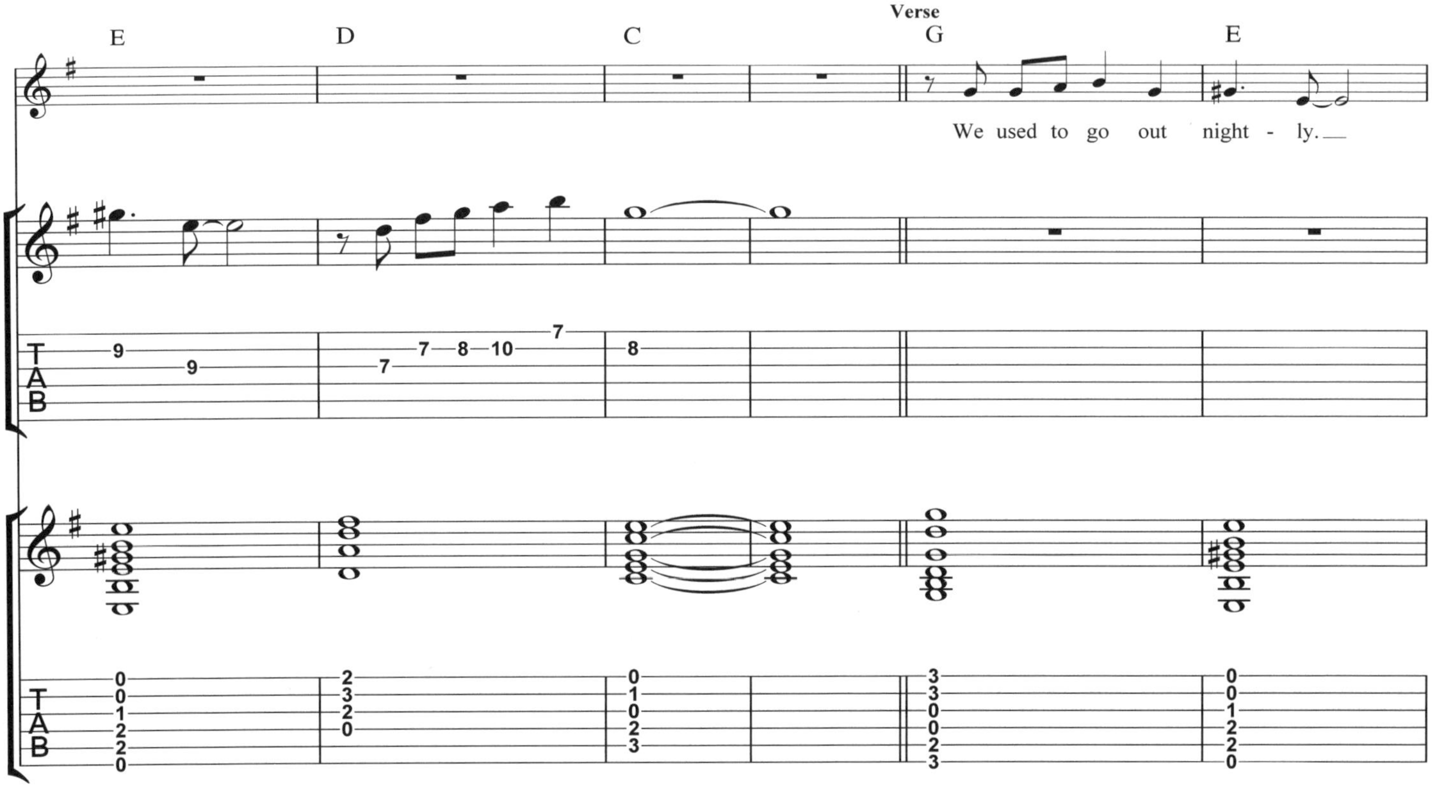

E
D
C
Verse
G
E
We used to go out night - ly.

G E G E
To the ar - mour - ies. You used to be my team mate.
D C F♯m
Or that's the way it seems. We lost our
A D
friends be - cause you want - ed to. They had no faith in you,
A F♯m
I had faith in you. You said we
TAB

A
D
don't need a - ny bod - y new. It's just me and you
C
E
on a bi - cy - cle for two. Ah ah
Verse
G
E
ah We used to hold on tight - ly.
G
E
G
E
And you re - lied on me. I used to be your team mate.

D
C
F#m
Or that's the way it seems.
We lost our
A
D
friends be - cause you want - ed to.
They had no faith in you,
A
F#m
I had faith in you.
We did
A
D
ev - 'ry - thing you want - ed to,
it was just me and you

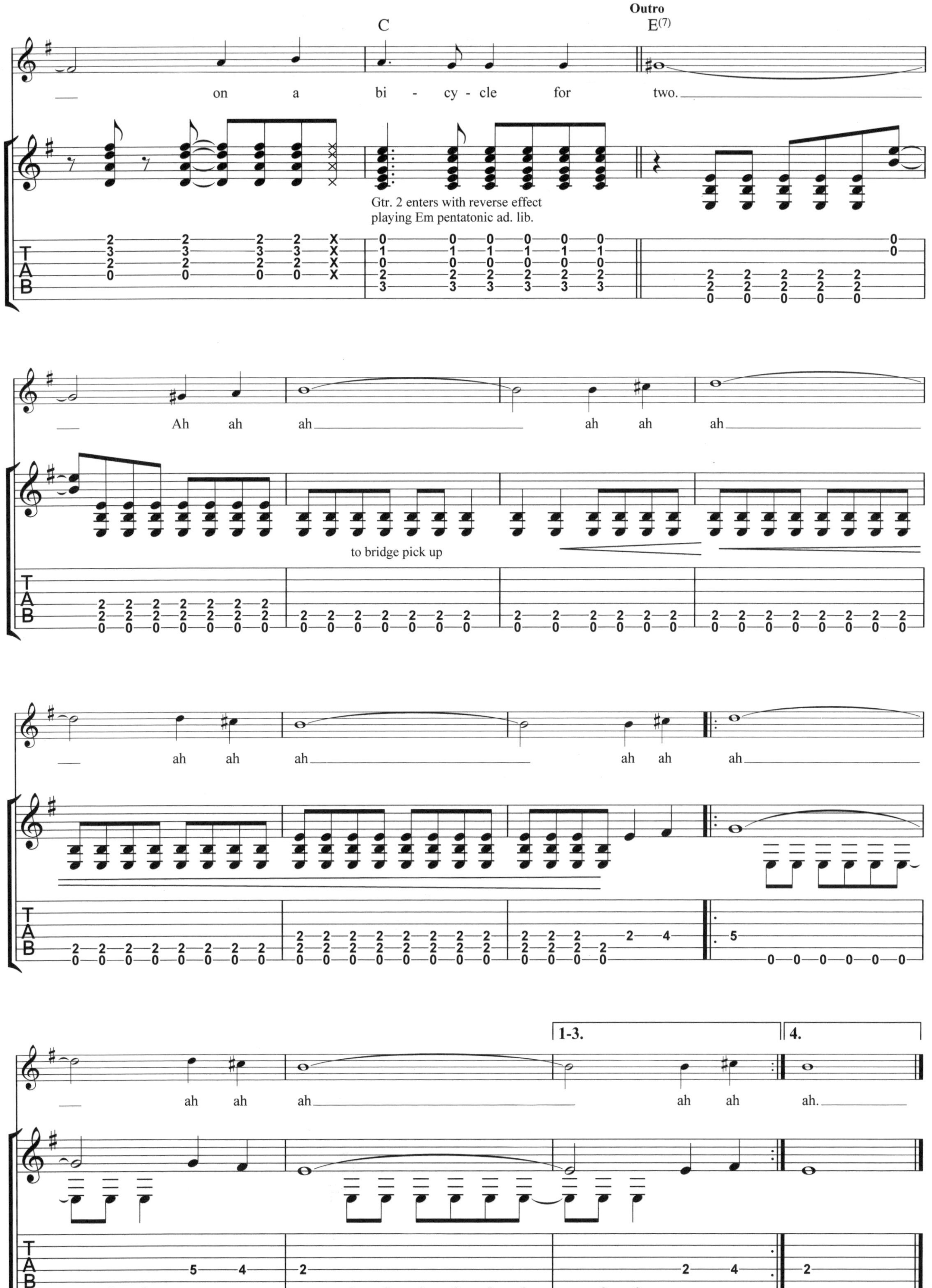
Outro
C
E(7)
on a bi - cy - cle for two.
Gtr. 2 enters with reverse effect playing Em pentatonic ad. lib.
Ah ah ah ah ah ah
to bridge pick up
ah ah ah ah ah ah
1-3.
4.
ah ah ah ah ah ah.

Guitar Tabalature Explained

Guitar music can be notated in three different ways: on a musical stave, in tablature, and in rhythm slashes

RHYTHM SLASHES are written above the stave. Strum chords in the rhythm indicated. Round noteheads indicate single notes.

THE MUSICAL STAVE shows pitches and rhythms and is divided by lines into bars. Pitches are named after the first seven letters of the alphabet.

TABLATURE graphically represents the guitar fingerboard. Each horizontal line represents a string, and each number represents a fret.

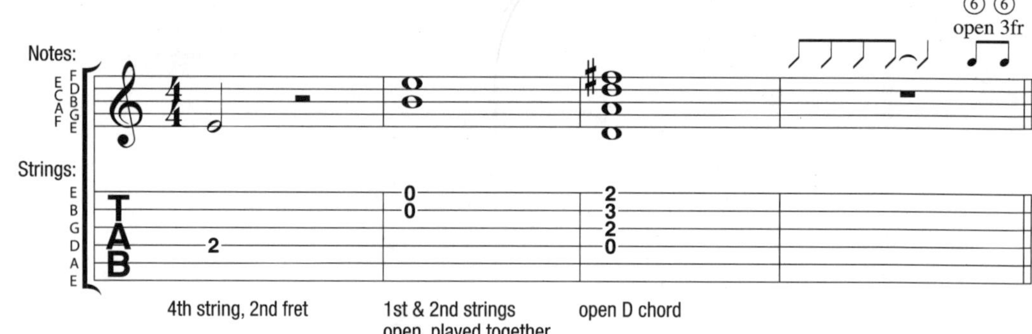

Definitions For Special Guitar Notation

SEMI-TONE BEND: Strike the note and bend up a semi-tone (1/2 step).

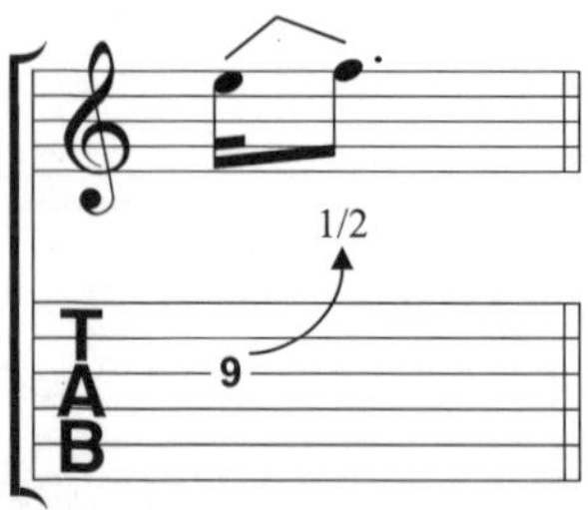

WHOLE-TONE BEND: Strike the note and bend up a whole-tone (whole step).

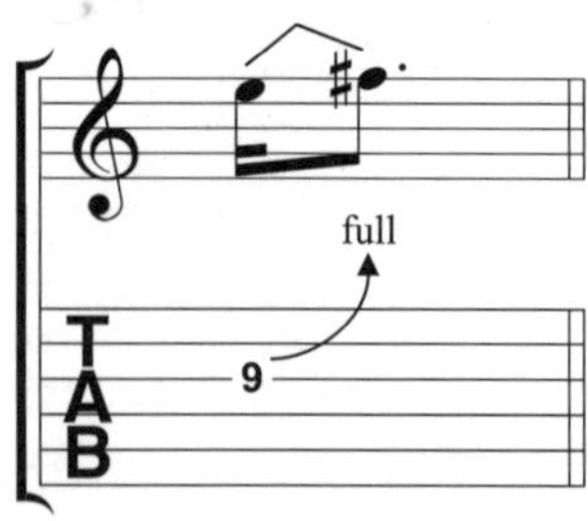

GRACE NOTE BEND: Strike the note and bend as indicated. Play the first note as quickly as possible.

QUARTER-TONE BEND: Strike the note and bend up a 1/4 step.

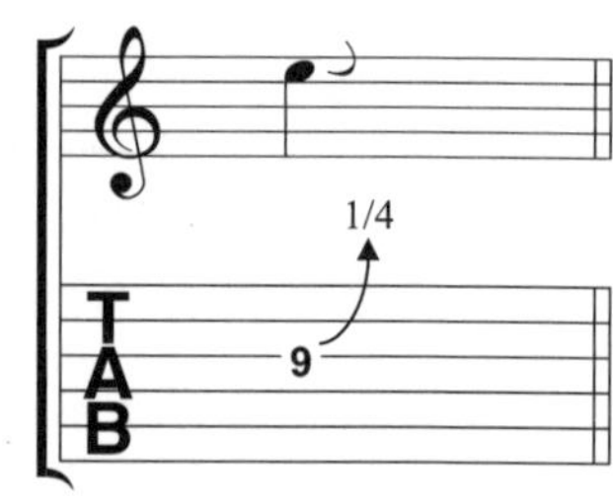

BEND & RELEASE: Strike the note and bend up as indicated, then release back to the original note.

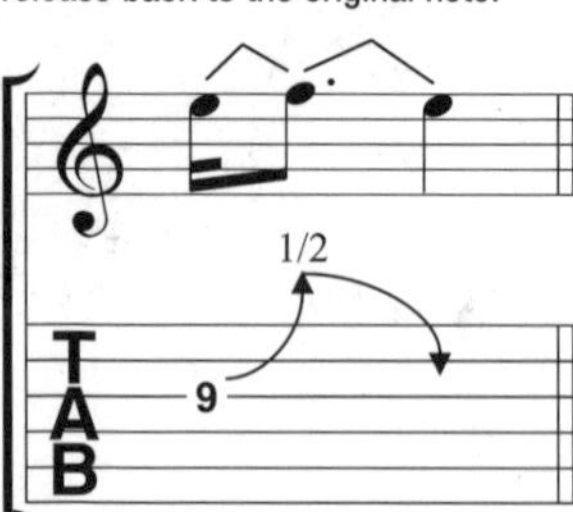

COMPOUND BEND & RELEASE: Strike the note and bend up and down in the rhythm indicated.

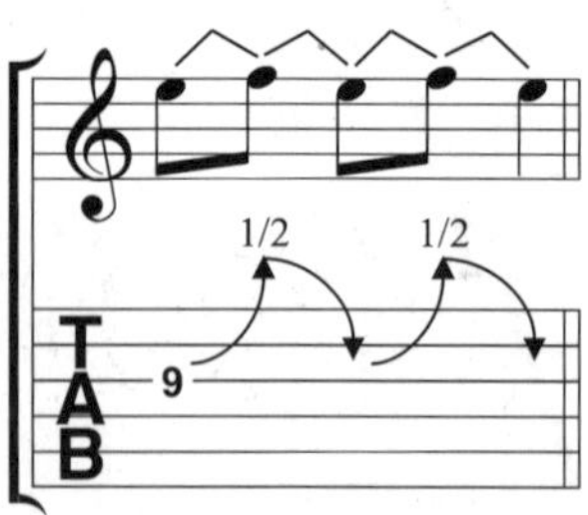

PRE-BEND: Bend the note as indicated, then strike it.

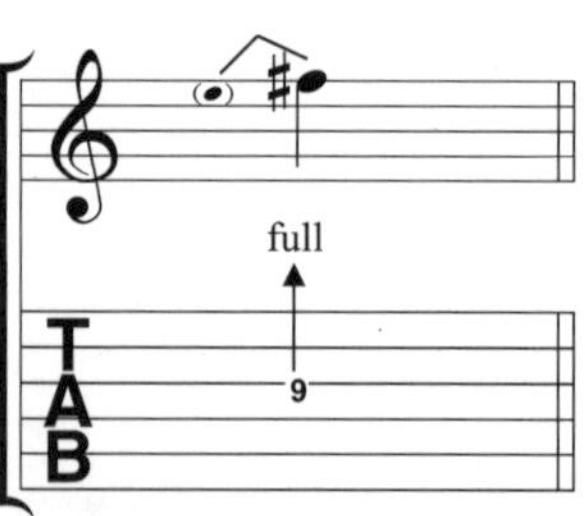

PRE-BEND & RELEASE: Bend the note as indicated. Strike it and release the note back to the original pitch.

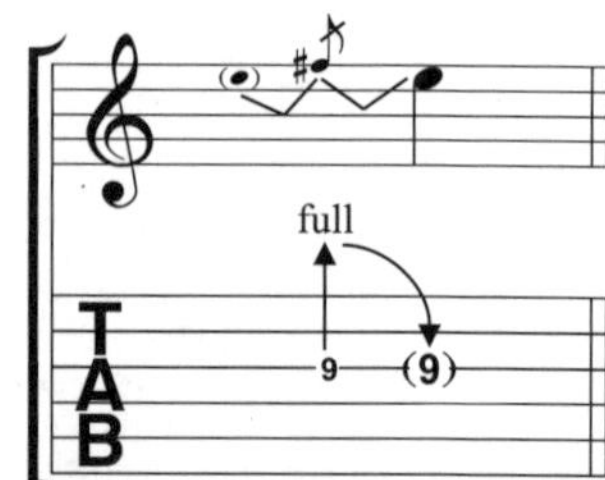

HAMMER-ON: Strike the first note with one finger, then sound the second note (on the same string) with another finger by fretting it without picking.

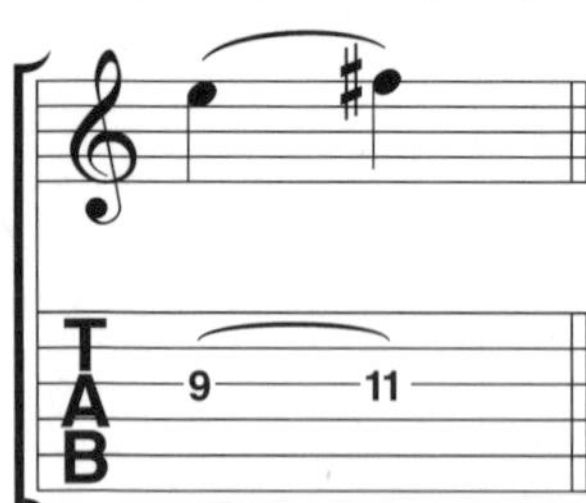

PULL-OFF: Place both fingers on the notes to be sounded, strike the first note and without picking, pull the finger off to sound the second note.

LEGATO SLIDE (GLISS): Strike the first note and then slide the same fret-hand finger up or down to the second note. The second note is not struck.

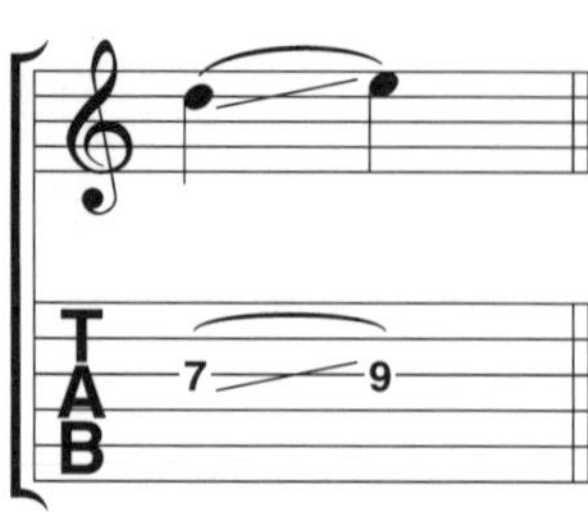

MUFFLED STRINGS: A percussive sound is produced by laying the fret hand across the string(s) without depressing, and striking them with the pick hand.

NATURAL HARMONIC: Strike the note while the fret-hand lightly touches the string directly over the fret indicated.

PICK SCRAPE: The edge of the pick is rubbed down (or up) the string, producing a scratchy sound.

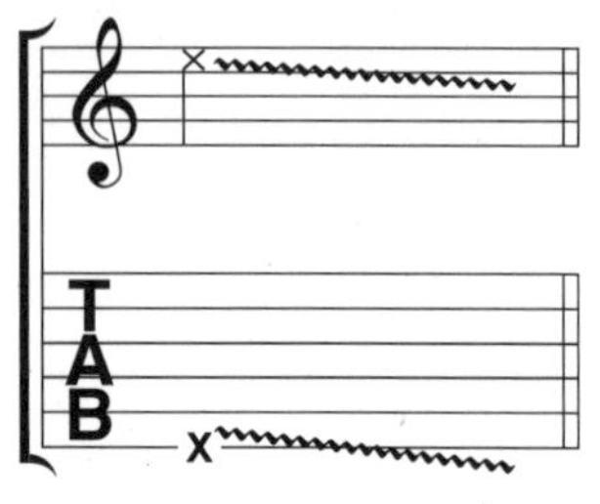

PALM MUTING: The note is partially muted by the pick hand lightly touching the string(s) just before the bridge.

SHIFT SLIDE (GLISS & RESTRIKE): Same as legato slide, except the second note is struck.

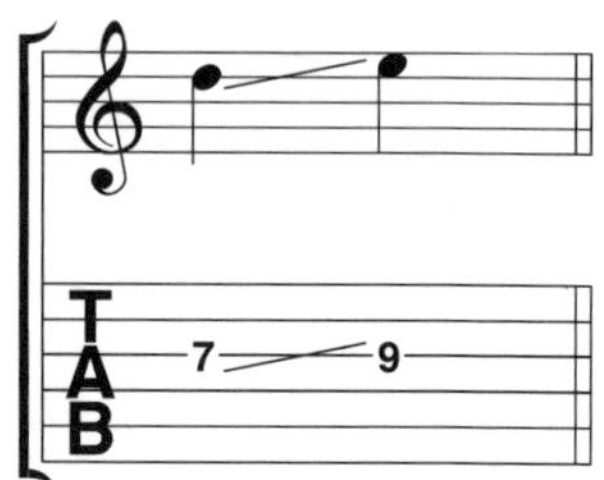

NOTE: The speed of any bend is indicated by the music notation and tempo.